LIFESTART

LIFESTART

A BASIC SURVIVAL GUIDE

JOHN ANDERSON

John Murray

Related titles published by John Murray include the *Basic Skills* series:

English by Paul Groves and Nigel Grimshaw
Arithmetic by John Deft
Electronics by Tom Duncan
Health, Hygiene and Safety by Di Barton and Wilf Stout
Science by Peter Leckstein

© John Anderson 1988

First published 1988
by John Murray (Publishers) Ltd
50 Albemarle Street, London W1X 4BD

Designed and typeset by
Gecko Limited, Bicester, Oxon.
Printed in Great Britain by
The Alden Press, Oxford

British Library Cataloguing in Publication Data

Anderson, John
    Lifestart.
    1. Great Britain. Careers Choice. – For school leavers
    I. Title
    331.7′02′0941

ISBN 0–7195–4447–5

CONTENTS

Note to the reader

Every effort has been made to achieve accuracy, but readers are recommended to confirm details with the relevant body.

Much of the information and advice given in this book depends on your knowing the addresses of bodies you need to contact. The logo

refers to the 'Addresses' section at the back of the book, starting on page 183.

Acknowledgements

The author would like to thank the following:

John Cleese and Connie Booth for permission to quote an extract from the BBC television programme, *Fawlty Towers* (p. 65); Leon Griffiths and Willow Books for the quotations from *Arthur Daley's Guide to Doing it Right*; the Family Planning Information Service for the diagrams from which those on p. 129 were adapted; the BBC for the A,B,C concept from the BBC television programme, *Save a Life* (pp. 143–4).

Photographs
The Kobal Collection (pp. 1, 9, 29, 49, 59, 70, 78, 82, 85, 97, 101, 108, 117, 124, 134, 142, 148, 153, 165, 172); the United Nations Information Centre, London (p. 181); the United States Army Audio Visual Agency, Washington D.C. (p. 181).

Cover photograph of the New York Marathon passing over Brooklyn Bridge by Steve Krongard, courtesy of the Image Bank.

OPTIONS

You CAN get skills, experience and qualifications.

Whether you're at school (in third, fourth, fifth or sixth year), training, unemployed, at college, working, disabled, fed up, or just looking for something to do, now's the time to pick up the right skills for work and life.

WHY ▶▶▶

Why bother to choose courses and learn skills? Many people say that once you're in work it's toughness, determination, hard work, and maybe a bit of luck that matter more than anything else.

People who learn skills are more likely to get work and make a success of life outside work than those who don't bother. And

All addresses in Addresses!

1

with skills, work and life will be more interesting and satisfying, with more money and better prospects.

Boring? Not if you choose what, where and how to learn to suit yourself. Work experience, new and exciting school and college courses, radio and TV programmes, evening classes, volunteering, overseas expeditions ... there are lots of opportunities to pick up skills, including vital skills that can't be tested in an exam: dealing with people, making decisions, job-finding, staying fit.

Many opportunities are free; on some courses *they* pay *you*!

And whatever, wherever and however you choose to learn, it's a great opportunity to meet people, challenge yourself, become more confident, take a new look at the world, and have some fun too!

USELESS? ▶▶▶

Not clever enough? Useless at exams? Failed everything? Don't want to fail again?

No problem. Learning is a skill you can learn!

SECRETS

- ignoring anyone who tries to put you down, or doesn't know how good you are
- remembering the skills you have already (right now you're reading, and that's a skill that thousands of people in this country don't have)
- choosing *enthusiastic teachers*, who show you what you *can* do
- choosing what, where and how to learn, and knowing why you're taking a course, so that you're an *enthusiastic learner*
- taking clear and simple notes which help you to think, understand, remember and revise
- perhaps choosing a course without an exam: some courses give you a certificate for what you can do, instead of judging you as a 'pass' or 'fail'
- having a bash, and then, if necessary, another bash! You can resit exams or, like many people, you may do better if you choose new subjects

- organisation: for example, keeping notes and files in good order
- planning: for example, making daily and weekly timetables for revision and study
- writing essays with an introduction (kicking the ball in the direction you want to go); five to ten different points, one per paragraph, in a logical order (tackling); and finally drawing it all into a conclusion (scoring the goal)
- asking for help: many teachers, supervisors and employers are so fed up with people who don't bother to learn that they'll do anything they can to help you; also ask them to arrange the courses *you* want; after all, you're the customer.
- taking a course to learn how to learn (study skills, essay writing, revision . . .)
- taking regular breaks (for sport, hobbies, meeting friends)

and so on.

READING

- study and revision aids in many bookshops (from Letts, Pan, Penguin, Kogan Page)
- *Teach Yourself* . . . series (Hodder and Stoughton)
- *Made Simple* . . . series (Heinemann)
- *Success In* . . . series (John Murray)
- *How to Pass Exams* (Unwin)

YOU ▶▶▶

First, what about you?

NEEDS

It would make your choice of subjects a lot easier, and allow you to make a much better choice, if you started to choose the *sort* of career you would like (see page 49). It's also worth thinking about subjects that could be useful for life in general (e.g. for bringing up a family, using leisure time, coping with unemployment).

LIKES

If you like a subject, you may do well at it.

3

ABILITIES

If you do well at a subject, it could be a confidence booster to help get you through other subjects.

OPPORTUNITIES ▶▶▶

Do you know *all* the subjects open to you (see page 6), and *all* the opportunities to take them (see page 9)? You may or may not have much choice until 16, that depends on your school, but after that there's a fantastic choice. It's a pity to miss out just because you don't know about an opportunity.

> ▶ '**I was useless at school, and beaten in every exam by the class swot. That guy was brilliant and he became an accountant. And I employ three of those.' (Michael Caine, British film star and millionaire)** ◀

CHOOSING ▶▶▶

ADVICE

Vital. For example, if you're choosing science subjects for some careers, you may have to think double, e.g. maths *and* physics. Or if you're choosing a practical course for a particular job, you have to double check whether the qualification it leads to is accepted by employers. Local careers officers and school careers teachers are your best contacts. For information about each course, speak to subject teachers, supervisors, lecturers, heads of departments, and trainees or students already taking the course.

RIGHT

The right choice is the choice that's right for *you*. Although you need all the advice you can get, only *you* can make the right choice. It can be a disaster to allow yourself to be pushed into the wrong course by teachers, friends or parents. After all it's you who has to do all the training or studying!

It can also be a disaster to push yourself into the wrong course. You don't have to do what 'everybody else' is doing, because there is no 'everybody else':
- there are 13, 23, 33, 83 year olds learning how to read and write, taking GCSEs and getting degrees
- there are women learning engineering, science, management and heavy lorry driving
- there are men learning nursing, typing, languages and child care
- there are blind students at university

and so on.

WHAT

English and maths (even at a basic level) are vital for most careers and courses. After that the experts' advice is: 'don't put all your eggs in one basket.' In many other countries everyone takes more subjects than we do, and a better mixture (balance) of different *types* of subject. This allows them to choose all sorts of careers and courses later on, and gives them better all-round skills to fall back on. It looks as though we'll have to start doing that (see page 51).

SCHOOL OPTIONS

Groups	Subjects (Examples)
English	English and English language
Maths	arithmetic and maths
Physical	physical education and sport
Practical	craft, design and technology, art, drama, home economics
Language	French, German, Spanish, Latin
Science	physics, chemistry, biology, integrated sciences
Arts	history, English literature, geography, social studies
New	parentcraft, food and nutrition, computer studies

A good balance means choosing at least one subject from each group

CHOOSING DIFFERENT TYPES OF SKILL

Skill	Why (examples)	Subjects (examples)	
Survival	coping	English	asserting
	choosing	arithmetic	yourself
	finding out	work	careers
	confidence	form-filling	managing money
	fitness	health	social education
	dealing with people	job-finding	problem-solving
		parentcraft	adventure
		relationships	training
		sports	physical
		drama	education
		safety	coping with
		using leisure	unemployment
		learning	computers
		(reading, writing	work experience
		listening and	communication
		speaking)	
		religious studies	
Practical	making	typing	motor vehicle
	operating	soccer	studies
	designing	nursing	photography
	performing	driving	farming
	selling	engineering	(agriculture)
	handling	needlework	music
		metalwork	floristry
		computing	business
		catering	design
		sea fishing	word processing
		caring	sign-writing
		plumbing	drama
		building	art
		accountancy	hairdressing
Academic	calculating	history	physics
	describing	Latin	economics
	judging	literature	sociology
	analysing	chemistry	modern studies
	debating	biology	astronomy
	researching	government	geography
		mathematics	Russian

The right number of courses to take is the number that neither overstretches nor understretches you. Employers prefer people with four good grades, instead of eight poor grades, or one excellent grade.

At 16, what, where and how to learn depend on you. The right choice makes all the difference. Some people prefer on-the-job training for the money and to get away from college. Some find a college of further education the ideal answer if they're fed up with school, but still keen to get more qualifications. Many mix the two in Youth Training. Some prefer the slower pace of part-time courses at college or home. Some travel the world for experience and adventure.

CAN'T?

Can't choose? Don't panic! Remember
- *you can* keep your options open by choosing a good mixture of courses which allow you to choose all sorts of careers and courses later on
- *you can* find out which skills you need by working (e.g. work experience from school/college, a Saturday job, a holiday job, or volunteering)

NEXT

If you're deciding on courses outside school you need to know:
- whether you need skills, qualifications (and certain grades) or experience first (see page 25)
- where, when, and how to apply (see page 26)
- how to get any money you need (see page 27)
- whether you can take the course part-time (see page 28)
- whether to take a break first and come back fresh (see page 28)

CONTACTS
- careers officer at your local careers office (see phone book under 'Careers' or under the name of your local council; in Northern Ireland the careers office is at your local Jobmarket): you can see a careers officer whether you're at school, college, training, working or unemployed
- careers teacher at school.

READING

- *Which Way Now* (Careers and Occupational Information Centre (COIC)): booklet given away free each year (also listen out for special programmes on Radio 1)
- *Decisions at 13/14+* (Careers Research and Advisory Centre (CRAC))
- *Decisions at 15/16+* (CRAC)
- *Decisions at 17/18+* (CRAC)

OPPORTUNITIES

WHAT
WHERE
APPLYING
MONEY
TIME
BREAKS

Whether you want to learn reading and writing, motorcycle maintenance, Latin, or astrophysics, you CAN!

Here are just some of the opportunities open to you. Many are open to people of all ages, so you've got plenty of second chances after school, and opportunities to keep updating your skills throughout your life.

WHAT ▶▶▶

All of these opportunities can lead to courses at the next level. You *may* need general level qualifications to do further level courses, and further level qualifications to do higher level courses. *Or maybe not.* You can, for example, take a degree with no qualifications at all.

All addresses in Addresses!

9

LEVELS OF SKILL

Level	What (examples)	Where (examples)
Basic	Basic Skills Foundation Programme AEB Basic Test TVEI CPVE/SCOTVEC National Certificate Youth Training on-the-job training special skills RSA	school group training centre work college of further education home adult education centre
General	GCSEs/Scottish Standard Grades CPVE/SCOTVEC National Certificate Youth Training apprenticeship on-the-job training RSA City and Guilds BTEC/SCOTVEC First special skills	school training centre work college of further education sixth form college home adult education centre private centre
Further	RSA City and Guilds BTEC/SCOTVEC National A level/Scottish Higher	school college of further education sixth form college home
Higher	BTEC/SCOTVEC Higher National professional degree	home special college college of higher education polytechnic/Scottish central institution university

BASIC SKILLS

What
- help with everyday skills for work and life

10

Subjects

- reading and writing (literacy – see the Adult Literacy logo below), using numbers (numeracy), dealing with people, using the phone, staying fit, managing money, choosing careers, form-filling, job-finding, learning . . .

Who

- anyone

Why

- one in ten school-leavers (and about two million adults) have problems with reading and writing (illiteracy)
- many people have problems using numbers, keeping fit, keeping out of debt, finding work, getting on with people . . .
- you'll be given every help to succeed

FOUNDATION PROGRAMME

What

- certificates awarded after two-year courses (in some schools)

Subjects

- to do with work involving people, technology, arts and design and money

Who

- 14–16 year olds

Why

- awarded by BTEC and City and Guilds
- work experience outside school
- as well as, or instead of, GCSE
- a certificate saying what you *can* do

AEB BASIC TESTS

What

- certificates awarded by the Associated Examining Board (AEB)

Subjects

■ health, hygiene and safety, arithmetic, English, geography, computer awareness . . .

Who

■ anyone

Why

■ as well as, or instead of, GCSE

TVEI

What

■ Technical and Vocational Education Initiative courses (not in Scotland)

Subjects

■ keyboarding, electronics, design, photography, child care, commerce, media, tourism, construction, catering, computing, graphical communications, marketing . . .

Who

■ 14–18 year olds

Why

Good:

■ more you, less teacher
■ brings subjects alive
■ work at your own speed
■ learning by doing

■ also a chance to work for GCSE, RSA, City and Guilds, BTEC qualifications
■ work experience out of school

Bad:

■ may not get a good mixture of skills unless you choose other options too

GCSEs AND SCOTTISH SCE STANDARD GRADES

What

■ General Certificate of Secondary Education

- Scottish Certificate of Education
- replacing CSE, GCE and Scottish O Grades
- one- or two-year courses depending on where you take them

Subjects

- exams in most traditional school subjects and other subjects such as motor vehicle studies, keyboarding applications, food and nutrition, business and information studies, art and design, and communication

Who

- anyone

Why

Good:
- open to everybody, not just 'academic' people
- needed and/or very useful for many careers and courses
- marks throughout the year, not just for final exam
- can tackle some subjects at different levels (to suit your ability)
- test your skill at understanding, and solving problems, not just remembering facts

Bad:
- have to work hard all year!
- may still be difficult for some people

CPVE AND SCOTTISH NATIONAL CERTIFICATE

What

- Certificate of Pre-Vocational Education (one year full time)
- in Scotland, modular courses leading to SCOTVEC National Certificate (the 16+ Action Plan)

Subjects

- arithmetic, careers, computers (core subjects), plus health, managing money, hairdressing, catering, child care, distribution, information technology, business, technology, leisure

Who

- at least 16 years old
- no qualifications needed

13

Why
- chance to try out different subjects and work
- work experience (at least three weeks)
- could also pick up GCSE, BTEC/SCOTVEC, City and Guilds, etc.
- a certificate of achievement saying what you *can* do

YOUTH TRAINING

What
- Youth Training Scheme (YTS)
- Youth Training Programme (YTP in Northern Ireland)
- at a training centre (as a trainee getting a training allowance) or in a real job (as an employee getting a wage)
- two years' training if you start at 16; one year at 17

Subjects
- office skills, bricklaying, drama, hairdressing, engineering, gardening, joinery, electrical, sea fishing, tourism, agriculture, plumbing, decorating, information technology, soccer, skills for self-employment . . . just about anything.

Who
- 16 or 17 year olds, or disabled up to 21

Why
Good:
- they pay you (at least £28.50 in 1987–8; employees may be paid more)
- work experience (no experience can mean no job)
- several weeks in a college of further education or training centre
- paid holidays
- you can leave if you find a job
- chance to try out different subjects and work
- chance to pick up City and Guilds, RSA, BTEC/SCOTVEC etc.
- employers include companies such as Marks & Spencer, IBM and British Aerospace, as well as local factories, shops and offices

14

Bad:
- low pay for real work
- trainees may not get as good a deal as employees (who may get more useful references or be offered their job afterwards)
- skills may not be useful
- employers prefer qualifications like GCSE, RSA, BTEC/ SCOTVEC etc.

APPRENTICESHIP

What
- three or four years' paid training with an employer
- harder to get these days (Youth Training taking over), but still the main form of training for some jobs

Subjects
- plumbing, plastering, hairdressing, printing, carpentry . . .

Who
- 16 or 17 year olds (usually)

Why
- real job
- paid (but maybe not as much as ordinary workers)
- chance to take college courses to pick up City and Guilds, BTEC/SCOTVEC etc.

ON-THE-JOB TRAINING

What
- training in a real job

Subjects
- depends on job (but includes: dealing with people, using the phone, settling into working routine etc.)

Who
- 13 year olds for some part-time work
- 15 year olds for school work experience
- 16 year olds or older for other jobs

15

Why

Good:
- paid (volunteers can get benefits)
- can take part-time college courses (see page 27)
- two weeks' work experience could be worth a year at school!

Bad:
- pay may be low
- may have no qualifications when you leave
- school rules replaced by work rules
- training may be short and poor
- part-time learning not easy
- might be choosing a career too early

SPECIAL SKILLS

What

- full-time, part-time and spare-time courses offered by colleges of further education, youth groups, government training schemes (see page 89), unemployment centres . . .

Subjects

- motor maintenance, choosing careers, shorthand, child care, job-finding, writing essays, using leisure time, coping with unemployment, French, Gaelic, Welsh, Irish, photography, book-keeping, management, information technology, plumbing, women's studies, sports, typing, maths, self-defence, word processing, catering, drama, art, politics, craftwork, self-employment (even at school: see page 77), bricklaying, decorating, learning to play a musical instrument, computer programming, gardening, health . . .

Who

- at least 16 for courses outside school
- at least 18 and unemployed for some government schemes (but there are exceptions)
- you don't need any qualifications

Why

- may get a qualification
- may be paid a training allowance on a government scheme

RSA

What
- certificates and diplomas from the Royal Society of Arts
- courses at all levels (including courses you can take at school)

Subjects
- using numbers, English, maths, English as a second language, telephonist/receptionist skills, typing, word processing, book-keeping, commerce, retail distribution, languages . . .

Who
- anyone

Why
- needed and/or very useful for many careers

CITY AND GUILDS

What
- certificates from the City and Guilds of London Institute (CGLI)

Subjects
- agriculture, engineering, construction, information technology, hotel and catering, hairdressing . . .

Who
- At least 16 years old

Why
- needed and/or very useful for many careers

BTEC/SCOTVEC

What
- certificates and diplomas from the Business and Technical Education Council

- certificates and diplomas from the Scottish Vocational Education Council
- at general (First), further (National) and higher (Higher National) levels

Subjects
- technology, science, agriculture, secretarial studies, sea fishing, retail distribution, caring, forestry, business, printing, computing, design, catering . . .

Who
- at least 16 years old

Why
- needed and/or very useful for many careers and courses

A LEVELS AND SCOTTISH HIGHERS

What
- one or two year courses depending on where you take them

Subjects
- many school subjects and others including government and political studies, ancient history, sociology, technical design and graphical communications, history and appreciation of art . . .

Who
- anyone

Why
- needed and/or very useful for many careers and courses

PROFESSIONAL

What
- further and higher level qualifications for certain careers

Subjects
- nursing, accountancy, social work, law . . .

18

Who
■ anyone with the right further or higher level qualifications

Why
■ needed for many specialised careers

DEGREE

What
■ two, three and four year full-time or part-time courses leading to qualifications such as the Diploma of Higher Education, DipHE (a new and popular two year course); Bachelor of Arts (BA); Bachelor of Science (BSc) etc.

Subjects
■ engineering, business, drama, design, computer science, chemistry, English, biology, history, economics, law, physics, nursing, graphic design, astronomy, teaching, architecture, music, communications studies, youth and community work, hotel and catering, tourism, recreation, sports studies . . .

Who
■ you don't need any qualifications for the Open University (but you have to be at least 18)
■ you need further level qualifications (e.g. BTEC/SCOTVEC National, A levels, or Scottish Highers) for other colleges

Why
■ needed and/or very useful for many careers

SCHOOL

What
■ state and private schools/colleges

Why

Good:
- may enjoy school
- may have friends there
- can keep your options open a bit longer

Bad:
- waste of time if you don't know what you're doing (may leave it too late to get Youth Training or an apprenticeship)
- may be fed up with school
- can't do certain subjects
- may not be treated as an adult

GROUP

What

- travel and adventure group (see page 159)
- Unemployment Centre (see page 83)
- leisure centre
- sports club
- school/college club
- self-help group (see page 147)
- friends (swopping skills)
- Duke of Edinburgh Award Scheme (see page 150)
- youth group, e.g. at a YMCA (see page 148)

Why

- getting away from classrooms and training centres

TRAINING CENTRE

What

- government, company and other training centres
- also Information Technology Educational Centres (ITECs)

Why

- the right training equipment
- approved training

WORK

What

- employment (see page 59):

20

ordinary full-time or part-time employment
Saturday and holiday jobs
a few weeks' work experience from school (if you can get your
headteacher or careers teacher to arrange it)
Community Programme: if you are unemployed (ask at the
Jobcentre)
even offering to work for nothing, if you want skills to set up
your own business
- self-employment (see page 70)
- volunteering (see page 78)

Why

Good:
- the real thing
Bad:
- without qualifications you could be exploited

COLLEGE OF FURTHER EDUCATION

What

- includes colleges of technology, technical colleges, colleges
  of business studies etc.

Why

Good:
- huge choice of courses
- freedom
- don't have to be in at nine!
- new friends
- adult atmosphere
- part-time courses
- wear what you like
- college life

Bad:
- not paid
- not so easy to keep your
  options open
- too relaxed for some people

SIXTH FORM COLLEGE

What

- for 16–19 year olds from various schools

21

Why

Good:
- wider choice of subjects
- more adult atmosphere
- meet new people
- clubs, discos . . .

Bad:
- waste of time if you don't know what you're doing (may leave it too late to get Youth Training or an apprenticeship)
- not paid
- choice of subjects may be limited to GCSE and A level type subjects

HOME

What

- radio and TV programmes: there's a huge choice, day and night, including schools programmes and the new Open College programmes
- lessons posted to you by a correspondence college: for example the National Extension College (basic, general and further level courses) and the Open University (general, further and higher level courses)
- teach yourself books: see page 3

Why

Good:
- don't need any qualifications first
- a way to *use* unemployment
- can study for qualifications (GCSE, A levels etc.) as an outside (private/external) candidate
- could learn anywhere (home, prison, abroad . . .)
- learn in your spare time and at your own pace

Bad:
- need self-discipline or it could be a waste of time
- may be lonely
- postal courses can be expensive

ADULT EDUCATION CENTRE

What

- local council centres

- some schools/colleges during the afternoon and evening
- Workers Educational Association centres
- university and polytechnic evening classes

Why

- part-time opportunities
- cheap (may be very cheap if you're unemployed)

PRIVATE CENTRE

What

- offer a variety of courses (secretarial skills, driving, cooking, languages, weight-training . . .)

Why

Good:
- courses may be shorter
- may not need any qualifications

Bad:
- probably can't get a grant
- some very expensive
- some not very good

SPECIAL COLLEGE

What

- schools, colleges and academies for nursing, art and design, agriculture, music, acting . . .

Why

Good:
- many are well-respected

Bad:
- may not have the life of colleges offering a wide variety of courses

COLLEGE OF HIGHER EDUCATION

What

- smaller than polytechnics and universities

23

- also includes institutes of higher education and teacher training colleges
- offers a variety of diploma and degree courses

Why

- may ask for even lower grades than polytechnics
- may get more individual help

POLYTECHNIC/SCOTTISH CENTRAL INSTITUTION

What

- polytechnics in England, Wales and Northern Ireland
- Scottish Central Institutions and larger Scottish Colleges of Technology
- offer a variety of diploma and degree courses

Why

- training for work at least as much as general education
- ask for lower grades than universities
- more part-time courses than universities

UNIVERSITY

What

- all over the UK
- also the Open University
- offer a variety of diploma and degree courses

Why

- General education at least as much as training for work
- highly respected qualifications

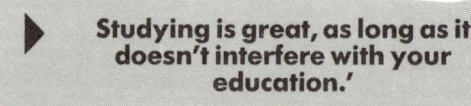

Studying is great, as long as it doesn't interfere with your education.'

Some courses have a closing date for applications many months or even a year before they begin. You may be able to apply late, but at best you'd be very lucky to get what you want (and where you want it). So, for example
- apply for apprenticeships when you're still at school
- apply for polytechnic/university in the autumn before the autumn when you want to start

Your choice of what and where to train/study will affect the next few years of your life. Shop around instead of taking the first thing you see or are offered. Try to visit, speak to supervisors/lecturers and trainees/students, and ask tough questions:
- how many people get a job afterwards?
- what does the training/course include?
- will it lead to a nationally recognised qualification?
- is it possible to take time off (e.g. to look for work or take a part-time college course)?
- is the course approved by a body such as the government or the local education authority or the Council for the Accreditation of Correspondence Colleges? (Ask for proof)
- what are the facilities like (canteen, library, sports centre, residences etc.)?
- what's the life like (clubs, discos . . .)?
and so on.

CONTACTS
- local careers officer
- school careers teacher
- local Jobcentre: details of all government schemes
- nearest Education Guidance Service
- youth workers
- teachers, supervisors, lecturers, heads of departments (a chat will improve your chances of getting in)
- local library: details of many local courses
- local council Education Department: details of local adult/community education courses at Adult Education Centres
- local Workers Educational Association (WEA) (see phone book)
- National Bureau for Handicapped Students: information about college facilities, access, help etc.

25

- National Association for the Care and Resettlement of Offenders (NACRO) (SACRO Scotland; NIACRO Northern Ireland)

🏫 READING

Prospectuses, booklets and books in your local school, college, careers office and Jobcentre library, including:
- *Action for jobs* (also free from your local Jobcentre/ Jobmarket)
- *Second Chances* (National Extension College (NEC))
- college prospectuses (you can also write to each college for a free copy)
- alternative student prospectuses (write to each students' union for a copy)
- Directory of Further Education (Careers Research and Advisory Centre (CRAC))
- *Student Book* (Macmillan): for higher level courses

MONEY ▶▶▶

Many courses are free, or very cheap, especially if you're under 19, or unemployed. If you need help with money, you can probably get it, even if you're at school, but apply months before you need help.

EDUCATION AUTHORITY

First, try to get a grant from your education authority. In England and Wales, that means from your county or district council's Education Department; in Scotland, your regional or island council Education Department and the Scottish Education Department (SED); in Northern Ireland, your area's Education and Library Board.

The size of the grant you can get depends on
- your needs: fees, accommodation, equipment etc.
- the level of course you are taking
- your parents' income (if they have to contribute to your grant, find out about covenanting)

There are two types of grant:
- money you *will* get if you are entitled to it (a 'mandatory' grant)

- money you *may* get whether you are entitled to an ordinary grant or not (a 'discretionary' grant)

ALSO

- benefits (see page 117)
- employers (see page 65)
- sponsorship: some organisations (e.g. large companies and the armed forces) offer extra money on top of your grant (but only for higher level courses), if your new skills would be useful to them (e.g. engineering), and you agree to work for them for a certain time afterwards
- scholarship/bursary: from some schools, colleges, and universities
- charities/trusts: but it's not easy to get money this way
- job: not much good if it takes up too much time or makes you too tired; there's a limit to how much you can earn on a grant; if you have to pay tax (see page 114), claim a tax rebate, as a student

CONTACTS

- local careers officer
- school careers teacher
- colleges

READING

- free booklets on student grants from your education authority
- *Covenants for Students* (a free leaflet from the National Union of Students (NUS)
- *Scholarships* (Careers and Occupational Information Centre (COIC))
- *Sponsorships* (COIC)
- *Directory of Grant-Making Trusts* (Charities Aid Foundation)
- free college prospectuses

TIME ▶▶▶

Full-time is easier, and it's easier to get a grant to do it. But you may be able to take a course part-time, or in your spare time; for example:

- one day or two half days off work, to do a college course (day release)

27

- several weeks or months off work, to do a college course (sandwich courses and block release)
- learning at home (see page 22)
- evening classes (e.g. at your local college of further education)

BREAKS ▶▶▶

Nights out, sports, holiday jobs, travel and volunteering are all an important part of learning.

If you have the offer of a place at a college, you may be able to wait a year before going. Some people find that this helps them to settle down to a course later on. Of course, if you don't have any work or travel organised first, it could be a waste of a year.

READING
- *A Year Off* (Careers Research and Advisory Centre (CRAC))
- *Jobs in the Gap Year* (Independent Schools Careers Organisation)

BASICS

YOU
PEOPLE
WRITING
PHONING
NUMBERS
INFORMATION
COMPUTERS

A few basic skills can make life and work a lot easier. And they could make the difference between getting, or not getting, a job.

Many are dealt with in separate chapters of this book, but here are a few of the most important ones.

YOU ▶▶▶

'I have more trouble with myself than any other person I know!' said one famous comedian. Attitudes can affect everything: personality, friendships, looks, moods, confidence, enthusiasm.

29

SECRETS

- *if you think you can, you can; if you think you can't, you can't; so why not think you can?*
- if you act enthusiastically, you become enthusiastic!
- the important thing is not where you are, but where you want to go
- if you aim for nothing, that's what you'll get!
- goals aren't much use if they're *unrealistic*
- it's enough to settle for what you *can* do
- organisation: for example, a few cheap cardboard files can help to keep letters, bills, notes, forms etc. in order
- planning: for example, a simple daily timetable can help to avoid the old trap of wasting hours in bed, arcades, pubs, in front of the TV, and then leaving important work until the last minute, when you're too tired to do it
- the action habit: everything starting *today*

and so on.

PEOPLE ▶▶▶

Obviously people are the most important part of anything. Dealing with people is a skill. It can make the difference between success and failure in just about anything.

SECRETS

- everyone matters: women and men, young and old, black and white, rich and poor, Catholic and Protestant, disabled and able-bodied . . .
- listening is more important than talking
- it's easy to put people down by words or actions; it takes a lot more sense not to
- co-operation saves aggravation
- a loud person who says too much, or a shy person who says too little, can seem rude, even if they don't mean to be
- a frosty reception may not be your fault; for example, older workers may feel threatened by younger workers; but in time things should work out
- if everyone is told what's going on, they feel involved, and are more likely to help
- people who are aggressive or shy may be hiding fears and problems that others don't know about

30

- everyone gets teased, especially new workers; a sense of humour is a big help
- looking, talking or acting like something from the Planet Zanussi can be mistaken for a lack of self-respect, or respect for others
- it helps to remember and use people's names; but many people (especially employers) prefer not to be called by their first name
- it saves a lot of hassle to deal with problems and complaints at the right time (e.g. immediately), and by speaking to the right people (e.g. a supervisor)
- politeness works wonders, and isn't crawling

and so on.

WRITING ▶▶▶

If it's well written, it shows that you're efficient. That can make the difference between getting or not getting a job, a customer's order, or a promotion.

LETTERS

- do a rough version first (the best letter writers often do this)
- type, or write very neatly
- stick to one shade of black or dark blue ink
- use clean, white, unlined paper (e.g. A4 size: 210×297mm)
- put your address, and the date, in the top *right*
- if you're writing to an official, put that person's name, organisation and any reference number, in the top *left*
- if you're not sure how to start, use 'Dear Sirs'
- keep it short (one side only, if possible)
- use simple language
- get to the point immediately, and stick to it
- make sure all points are clearly separated and in a logical order
- if there's more than one correction, rewrite the whole letter
- end with 'Yours faithfully' when you start with 'Dear Sir' or 'Dear Madam'
- end with 'Yours sincerely' when you start with 'Dear Mr' (Smith) or 'Dear Mrs' (Jones) or 'Dear' (Samantha)
- it's better to put your name in capital letters below your signature (in case your handwriting isn't clear)

31

- check (and ask someone else to check) spelling and grammar. Remember that the boss may expect you to correct his/her spelling!
- keep a copy or note of what you write, in case you're asked about it later on (e.g. at a job interview)
- remember that photocopied letters (e.g. for jobs) may go straight in the bin!
- use a long white or brown (manilla) envelope (about 220 × 110mm)
- if you need information, enclose an envelope (about 230 × 165mm) with your name, address and a stamp on it (stamped addressed envelope or SAE)
- see page 10

CRUMBLING, LEANING & DODGY
Estate Agents

27, Landslide Terrace, Falmouth, Cornwall, TR11 4ST.

11th November 1989

Mr. A. Daley,
Flash Office Furniture and Used Cars,
34, Lorryback Road,
LONDON,
SW6   3RE

Re: ADF 00001/89

Dear Mr. Daley,

Thank you for your letter of 10th November.

We are disappointed that you cannot fulfil our order for three 'Big Fish' executive swivel chairs in executive black. I am afraid that we cannot place an alternative order for the 'Beach Hustler' deck chairs as you suggest. We feel that tropical tangerine deck chairs would not be suitable for business purposes, even at a flood-damaged bargain price.

We look forward to receiving your Spring catalogue.

Yours sincerely,

Cliff Crumbling.

CLIFF CRUMBLING
Senior Partner

34, Sunset Boulevard,
Newcastle-upon-Tyne,
NE1 1TJ

3rd April 1989

Dear Sirs,

I would be grateful for a copy of the free Radio 7
booklet: 'Dealing with Difficult Parents.'

Please find enclosed a stamped addressed
envelope.

Yours faithfully

Amrik Singh

AMRIK SINGH

Mrs. N Smith,
Managing Director
Muck and Brass Ltd.,
356 - 358 East Road,
HALIFAX
West Yorkshire
HX1 2RT

FORM

- read it through first
- practise answers on a piece of paper (or photocopy)
- follow instructions at the top of the form
- type, or write very neatly
- stick to one shade of black or dark blue ink

- stick to the truth because you may be asked about what you write
- answer all questions fully, or explain why you can't
- if you run out of space, use an extra sheet, attached with a paper clip
- double check (and ask someone else to check) spelling and grammar
- keep a copy or note of what you write in case you're asked about it later on (e.g. at a job interview)
- see page 10

PUNCTUATION

Commas (,)

Show a slight pause between parts of the same sentence or list. Just say it to yourself and listen for any slight pauses:

U2 will be holding concerts in Cardiff, Liverpool, Belfast and Glasgow.

The England team are confident, but Brian Robson may not be fit in time for the match.

Aberdeen, Scotland's best team, are heading for Cup victory.

Quotation Marks (either ' or ")

Show that somebody said it or wrote it:

I said, 'Can I interest you in a suitcase full of wind-powered Mickey Mouse watches?'
'You're under arrest', he replied.

Apostrophes (')

Show missing letter(s), or that something belongs to something else:

I'd	say	there's	no such word as	can't
I would		there is		cannot

Coventry's best disco

Jane's bike

The Ulster players' best ever season
(after the 's' because there is more than one player)

34

But beware of classic bloomers such as:

you're (you are) confused with *your* (belonging to you)
it's (it is) confused with *its* (belonging to it)

Semicolons (;)

Show a longer pause than a comma but not as big a break as a full stop:

I fancy Lenny; he's into break-dancing.

Colons (:)

Show that you're giving more information:

There's a lot going on at the youth centre: snooker, table-tennis, a snack bar, and youth workers to help with any problems.

CONTACTS

- youth workers
- local careers officer
- school careers teacher
- local Citizens Advice Bureau
- whoever gives you a form; let them try to explain it!

READING

- books on letter-writing from your local bookshop
- a paperback dictionary such as the *Oxford Paperback Dictionary* (Oxford University Press)

WHAT ON EARTH?!

a/c	account
b/f	brought forward from the last calculation
c/o	care of (a temporary address)
C.O.D.	cash on delivery (you pay when it's delivered)
i.e.	that means
K	1000 of something (e.g. 5K meaning £5000)
MD	Managing Director
Ms	used by some women instead of Miss or Mrs
NB	very important
p.p.	on behalf of (e.g. before a secretary's signature on manager's letter)
re	with reference to (about)
rep.	a representative (e.g. visiting sales rep)
RSVP	please reply

audiovisual	you can hear it and see it
accounts	records of money paid or owed for goods or services
balance	what's left or owed after the calculation
clocking (on, off)	marking a card on a special machine when you arrive at/leave work
contract	agreement between buyer and seller
contractor	company employed to do a piece of work
credit note	note of money owed to a buyer (e.g. after returning goods)
dictaphone	mini tape recorder which records and plays back dictation
duplicator	hand operated machine for copying documents
estimate	calculated guess at the price
forenames	first/Christian names
franking machine	machine for marking letters with a postage mark, instead of a stamp
gross	before things such as tax, weight, costs etc. have been taken off
invoice	list of goods/services (and their prices) supplied to a buyer
negotiable	still to be agreed
net	after everything such as tax, weight, costs etc have been taken off
order	list of goods/services wanted by a buyer
petty cash	small amount of money kept for office coffee, stamps etc.
quotation	the real/fixed price
requisition	note asking for property or materials (e.g. from a stationery office)
retailer	shop selling goods to the public
shorthand	quick way of writing, using symbols instead of words
wholesaler	company storing goods from factories before reselling to shops

P H O N I N G ▶▶▶

Can be vital for getting a job, a customer's order, information …

PHONE

■ first jot down everything you want to say
■ if you're using a phone box bring plenty of coins or a phonecard
■ have all important information by your side: phones and extension numbers, names, dates of letters, job reference numbers, order numbers …
■ keep a pen and paper handy to jot down information

36

DIRECTORIES

Can be confusing:

- your local careers office is under the name of your local council (Jobmarket in N. Ireland)
- your local DHSS/Social Security Office is under Health and Social Security, Department of
- your local Department of Employment/Unemployment Benefit Office is under Employment, Department of
- your local Social Services Department is under the name of your local council
- your local Tax Office is under Inland Revenue

Phone: Disaster!

	(Phone rings)
Secretary	Yeah?
Mrs Narked	Is that Crumbling, Leaning & Dodgy?
Secretary	Yeah. Who's that then?
Mrs Narked	Mrs Narked. I would like to speak to Mr Luckless.
Secretary	Who?
Mrs Narked	(*loudly*) Mr Luckless! I'm phoning about the house you sent me to view on Tuesday, at 23 Gloom Villas. It's an absolute disgrace; I've nev...
Secretary	(*interrupting*) O.K. hang on love. I'll see if Tony's back from the pub. (*on internal phone*) Oh you're back; it's the phone.
Mr Luckless	Did the caller give a name and say what it's about?
Secretary	Oh it's someone on about some villa or something. I'll put it through anyway.
Mr Luckless	No wait a min . . .(*cut off*)
Secretary	Hello? You still there dear? (*puts her through*)
Mr Luckless	(*desperately trying all internal lines to find the call*) Hello? Hello? Hel . . .
Mrs Narked	&**XZi(+@§! rude X(%29=§ boozers £**1!2 shoddy $5%?½!! old ruin $')+!"£⅛!

Phone: Success!

	(Phone rings)
Secretary	Crumbling, Leaning & Dodgy. Good morning. Can I help you?
Mrs Narked	May I speak to Mr Luckless please?
Secretary	Mr Luckless. Yes certainly. May I have your name please?
Mrs Narked	Mrs Narked. I'm phoning about the house you sent me to view on Tuesday, at 23 Gloom Villas. It's an absolute disgrace; I've never seen anything so damp or dangerous in my life.
Secretary	*(speaking slowly to make sure he heard correctly and writing it all down)* Mrs Narked; and you're phoning Mr Luckless about 23 Gloom Villas, which you viewed on Tuesday. Thank you Mrs Narked. One moment please, I'll see if Mr Luckless is available.
	(on internal phone) Mr Luckless, this is Jeff. I have a Mrs Narked on the phone asking to speak to you about a house she viewed on Tuesday, at 23 Gloom Villas. She says it's damp and dangerous, and she sounds angry.
Mr Luckless	Thank you Jeff, I'll take it.
Secretary	It's on Line 5, Mr Luckless.
	(on outside line again) Hello Mrs Narked? Sorry to keep you. I'm putting you through to Mr Luckless now.
Mrs Narked	Oh . . . er . . . thank you *(calming down already)*
Mr Luckless	Hello Mrs Narked. I'm very sorry to hear of your complaint. Now may I suggest . . .

 'Where's your grammar?'
'In the front room watching TV.'

Don't panic! For most calculations nowadays we use calculators. But you should still be able to do basic sums, in case you don't have a calculator sometimes, or in some exams. Even with a calculator, you need a way of estimating the answer, in case you press the wrong button!

TIMETABLES

Midnight	00.00
1 am	01.00
8 am	08.00
Noon	12.00
1 pm	13.00
2 pm	14.00
7 pm	19.00
11 pm	23.00
1 minute past midnight	00.01
23 minutes past 8 in the morning	08.23
49 minutes past 5 in the afternoon	17.49
1 minute to midnight	23.59
and so on	

ADDING/SUBTRACTING

■ Working out the total cost of buying a record priced at £3.95 and a cassette at £5.13:

```
  3 . 95    (line up decimal points under each other)
+ 5 . 13    Work from column to column, starting from the right
£ 9 . 08    5 + 3 = 8: write 8
            9 + 1 = 10: remember the 1, write 0
            3 + 5 = 8: add the 1, write 9)
```

£9.08. Success!

■ Working out your score in a game of darts: you have to get 272 and with your next throw you score 43:

$\begin{array}{r} 272 \\ -\ 43 \\ \hline 229 \end{array}$

2 − 3 doesn't work: 'borrow' a 10 from the next column, making the 2 into 12

12 − 3 = 9: write **9**
You've taken 1 from the 7 in the tens column, so now treat it as a 6
6 − 4 = 2: write **2**
2 − 0 = 2: write **2**

229. Success!

1	2	3	4	5	6	7	8	9	10	11	12
2	4	6	8	10	12	14	16	18	20	22	24
3	6	9	12	15	18	21	24	27	30	33	36
4	8	12	16	20	24	28	32	36	40	44	48
5	10	15	20	25	30	35	40	45	50	55	60
6	12	18	24	30	36	42	48	54	60	66	72
7	14	21	28	35	42	49	56	63	70	77	84
8	16	24	32	40	48	56	64	72	80	88	96
9	18	27	36	45	54	63	72	81	90	99	108
10	20	30	40	50	60	70	80	90	100	110	120
11	22	33	44	55	66	77	88	99	110	121	132
12	24	36	48	60	72	84	96	108	120	132	144

100	e.g. £100
↑ × 10	
10	e.g. £10
↑ × 10	
1	e.g. £1
↑ × 10	
0.1	e.g. 10p
↑ × 10	
0.01	e.g 1p

MULTIPLYING

■ Working out your total pay after 10 weeks of Youth Training (at £28.50 a week):

multiplying by 10 moves the decimal point 1 number to the *right*

40

(multiplying by 100 moves it 2 numbers; by 1000 3 numbers etc.)

so 28.5 becomes 285.

£285.00. Success!

■ Working out the price of three pairs of socks at £1.24 each:

```
 124    (1.24 is the same as 124p)
× 3     3 × 4 = 12: carry the 1, write 2
───     3 × 2 = 6: add the 1, write 7
 372    3 × 1 = 3: write 3
```

372p or £3.72. Success!

■ Working out the sale price of jeans costing £15 with $\frac{1}{3}$ off:

$$\frac{1}{3} \times \frac{15}{1} \quad \frac{(1 \times 15)}{(3 \times 1)} = \frac{15}{3} \quad (15 \div 3) = 5$$

Subtract 5 from 15.

£10.00. Success!

DIVIDING

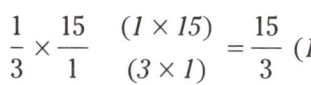

■ Splitting the cost of a £4.90 group ticket at the ice rink, between 10 in the group:

dividing by 10 moves the decimal point one number to the *left* (dividing by 100 moves it 2 numbers etc) 4.9 becomes .49

£0.49 or 49p. Success!

■ Splitting the cost of a gallon of minibus petrol at £1.82, between five people in a sports team:

```
    36 r2    (£1.82 is the same as 182p)
5)18²2      5 into 1 won't go
            5 into 18 goes 3 times and 3 left over: write 3 and
            carry 3 to the next column
            5 into 32 goes 6 times with 2 left over: write 6
            You can't split 2p between five people
```

36p each (but two people pay 37p). Success!

PERCENTAGES

Percentage is Latin for 'per 100'.
1% is 1 out of every 100 (or $\frac{1}{100}$).
33% is 33 out of every 100 (or $\frac{33}{100}$).

■ Adding 15% VAT to a customer's order costing £3:

$$\frac{15}{100} \times \frac{3}{1} \quad \frac{(15 \times 3)}{(100 \times 1)} = \frac{45}{100} \ (45 \div 100) = 0.45$$

add 0.45 to 3

£3.45. Success!

■ Adding a year's bank interest at 8% per year, to £50 kept in your account for a year:

$$\frac{8}{100} \times \frac{50}{1} = \frac{400}{100} = 4$$

add 4 to 50

£54. Success! (in the second year, 8% of £54)

AREA

■ Working out how much carpet you need for a bedroom measuring 3 × 4 metres:

$3 \times 4 = 12$

12 square metres. Success!

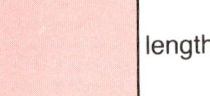

length

width

AREA = length × width

VOLUME

■ Working out the number of bricks in a pile 3 bricks high, 4 bricks long and 5 bricks wide:

$3 \times 4 \times 5 = 60$

60 bricks. Success!

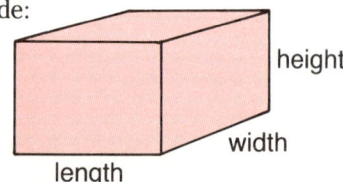

height

width

length

VOLUME = length × width × height.

AVERAGE

■ Working out West Ham's goal average after scoring 2, 0, 4, 1 and 3 goals on the first 5 Saturdays of the season:

$$\frac{10 \text{ goals}}{5 \text{ Saturdays}} = 2$$

2 goal average. Success!

GRAPHS

■ Making sense of a record shop's weekly LP sales figures, using a 'bar chart':
Paul Young 14
5 Star 25
U2 19
George Michael 10
Bananarama 29

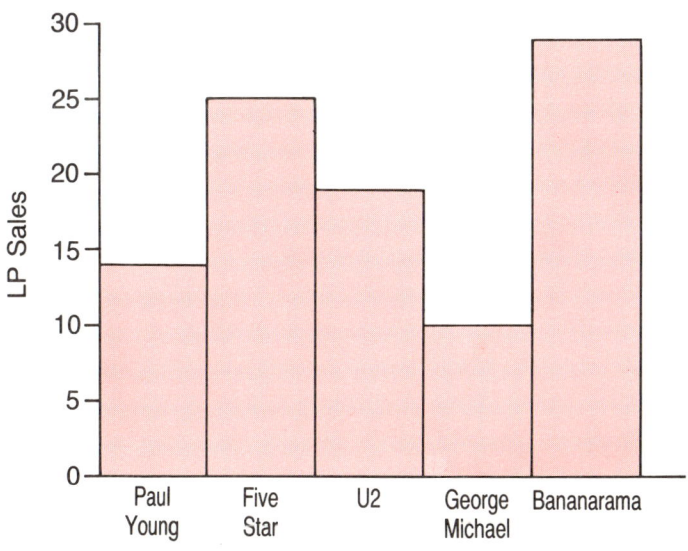

43

- Making sense of statistics about work in the mid 1980s, using a 'pie chart'
  people providing raw materials 3%
  people providing products 33%
  people providing services 64%

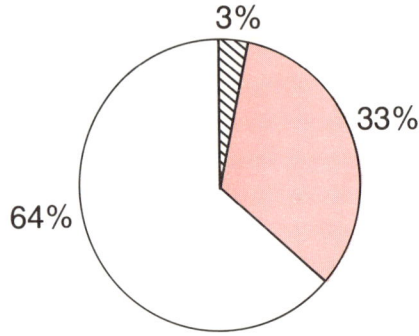

The %s must add up to 100%
The angles must add up to 360° (a circle)
So 1% = 3.6°

- Making sense of profit figures for a new business, using a 'line graph':
  1984 £2300
  1985 £3900
  1986 £2600
  1987 £3000
  1988 £4200

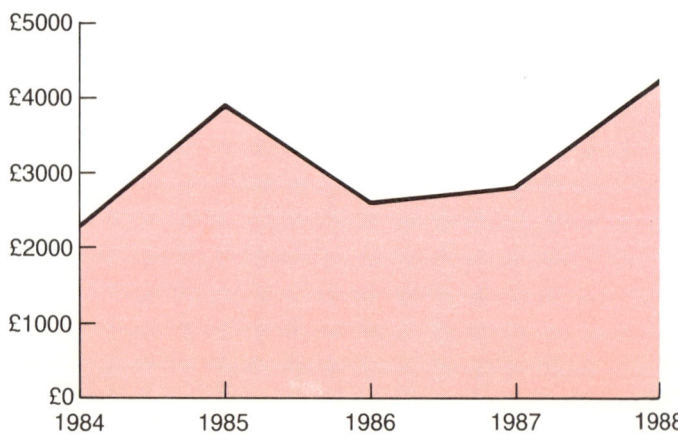

44

MEASUREMENTS

Length   1 foot (ft)   12 inches (ins)
            1 yard (yd)   3 feet (ft)
            1 mile   1760 yards (yds)

            1 centimetre (cm)   10 millimetres (mm)
            1 metre (m)   100 centimetres (cm)
            1 kilometre (km)   1000 metres (m)

Weights 1 pound (lb)   16 ounces (oz)
            1 stone   14 pounds (lb)
            1 hundredweight (cwt) 8 stones
            1 ton   20 hundredweight (cwt)

            1 gram (g)   1000 milligrams (mg)
            1 kilogram (kg)   1000 grams (g)
            1 tonne (t)   1000 kilograms (kg)

Area 1 square foot (ft^2)   144 square inches (sq. in)
         1 square yard (yd^2)   9 square feet (sq. ft)
         1 acre   4840 square yards (sq. yds)
         1 square mile (sq. mile) 640 acres

         1 square metre (m^2)   10,000 square centimetres (cm^2)
         1 hectare (ha)   10,000 square metres (m^2)
         1 square kilometre (km^2)   100 hectares

Capacity 1 pint (pt)   20 fluid ounces (fl. oz)
             1 gallon   8 pints (pt)

             1 centilitre (cl)   10 millilitres (ml)
             1 litre (l)   100 centilitres (cl)

Angles 360°   a circle
           180°   a straight line
           90°   a right angle

INFORMATION ▶▶▶

You stand a much better chance of getting information if you're clear about what you need, and ask for it clearly and simply, and in a way that encourages people to give it. For example, saying to an employer: 'have you got any jobs going?' is likely to get a 'yes' or 'no' reply, and probably 'no'. But saying 'I wonder if I could ask your advice about career opportunities in (whatever)', not only flatters the employer by asking him/her for advice, but also gives the employer time to think about vacancies and about you. Simple, but it could get you a job.

Writing, speaking, reading and listening are vital skills to learn. And the skill and habit of recording information in writing or on tape is an important one too.

Sources of information include:
- books
- newspapers
- Yellow Pages
- magazines
- libraries
- radio and TV
- noticeboards

- Citizens Advice Bureaus
- Law Centres
- friends
- parents
- experts
- gossip

and so on.

LIBRARY

Your local library is a goldmine of information: about jobs, hobbies, science, travel, skills, law, what's on, courses ... If you can't find the information you want, ask an assistant. You can also borrow books, records and cassettes, look at dictionaries, encyclopedias, atlases and telephone directories and read newspapers and magazines (new and old).

Books of facts (non-fiction) are shelved by number/subject from 000 to 999 such as:
- Careers 371
- Cooking 641
- Farming 630

- Computing 001
- Sports 790

If you know the author or title, look in the index, which may be small drawers full of cards, or a microfiche (microfilm) projector (a sort of slide projector which looks like a TV set) or a large book. If you can't find the book you want:
- check if it's in the special reference section or careers section
- ask a library assistant whether it has just been returned
- fill in a request card asking the library to keep it when a borrower returns it, or to get it from another library

If you want to take out books but haven't got a library ticket, bring some oficial identification which includes your name and address (e.g. a Medical Card), and apply for a ticket.

 CONTACTS

- National Youth Bureau
- Scottish Community Education Council
- Council for Wales of Voluntary Youth Services
- Youth Information Service, Belfast

 READING

If you live in Scotland, Wales or Northern Ireland, and want national information on the subjects in this book:
- *Young Scot* (Scottish Community Education Council)
- *On-Line* (Council for Wales of Voluntary Youth Services)
- *Young Ulster* (BBC Northern Ireland) in most libraries in Northern Ireland

COMPUTERS ▶▶▶

They're in homes, shops, warehouses, factories, libraries, banks, offices and studios, helping secretaries, managers, designers, librarians, detectives, journalists and car-builders to write letters, calculate wages, keep records, control machines, design products, keep accounts ... They're making work easier, quicker and more accurate.

Instead of working with pen and paper, you use a keyboard and TV screen (Visual Display Unit or VDU). The computer itself (linking the keyboard and screen) is a very fast adding machine that can also handle information such as words, numbers and pictures. It allows you to type in, correct, update, store, and find information, and (if it's attached to another machine such as a robot or printer) allows you to send out information (e.g. commands to robots, and words to printers).

Amazingly the computer can't do anything until it has been instructed (programmed) how, in every detail (just as you would tell a child). These instructions (programs) are typed in using a special language. One of the simplest languages is BASIC, which is very like ordinary English. A program can take hours to make, so many people buy them. You need a different program for whatever you're working on:
- for words (letters, documents ...): a word processing program
- for files (records, indexes ...); a data-base program

47

- for figures (accounts, plans . . .): an accounts package or a spreadsheet program
- for games (arcade, chess . . .): a games program

and so on.

The programs, and any information you are using, can be stored on magnetic tape (inside cassettes or plastic disks). One small cassette or disk can, for example, store this whole book.

CAREERS

WHY
HOPELESS?
YOU
WORK
CHOOSING

Whether you're at school (in third, fourth, fifth or sixth year), on
Youth Training, unemployed, at college or fed up with your job,
now's the time to start making the right choice of career.

WHY ▶▶▶

Why bother to choose careers? Unfortunately, choosing careers
can seem a crazy business: work may seem a long way off and
you may not have a clue what you want to do.

All addresses
in Addresses!

49

But it's a fantastic help just to *start* thinking about careers. You'll be miles ahead of all those who don't bother. And you can start training or studying with a goal to aim for.

Just a short time spent making the right choice of career could be repaid to you with years of interesting, challenging and satisfying work and life.

But why bother to work at all? Work can't offer everything (and it's important to have a life outside work), but it can give you:

- money
- fun
- confidence
- self-respect
- respect from others
- company
- something to do
- challenge
- achievement
- goals
  and so on.

H O P E L E S S ? ▶▶▶

No jobs? No qualifications? Things can be tough, but they're never hopeless.

SECRETS

- beating unemployment by choosing careers: if you know what you want, you're half-way to getting it
- looking at yourself, so that you know what sort of career you could stick at, and hopefully enjoy
- taking a look at *all* the opportunities open to you
- remembering that there are jobs (and courses) for people without qualifications

Y O U ▶▶▶

Whatever skills, experience, or qualifications you have or haven't got, you have something special to offer – *definitely*.

Perhaps it would help if you made a list called 'You' (like the one on page 57, using the list on page 52 for ideas) of words that best describe your interests, skills, personality and hopes.

Parents, friends, a local careers officer (see page 7) or school careers teacher may be able to help you to get a clearer picture of yourself. It's also worth asking your local careers officer or school careers teacher for a self-assessment questionnaire or special computer software which helps you to look at yourself in more detail. Obviously your interests, skills, personality and hopes change, so don't be too hard on yourself, or let others be too hard you.

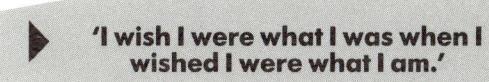

'I wish I were what I was when I wished I were what I am.'

WORK ▶▶▶

There are lots more careers to choose from than the ones you read about in one book or see at the local Jobcentre. Perhaps it would help if you made a list called 'Work' (like the one on page 57, using the list on page 54, and the books on page 54 for ideas) of work that roughly matches each of your interests, skills, personality and hopes.

Of course, as they say, 'things ain't what they used to be'. It's also worth thinking about the new world of work. Computers, cheap foreign goods and changes in what people are buying may mean that for many people work will no longer be a full-time job in one organisation for life. It may mean various jobs, with various employers, for various lengths of time, in various parts of the country, sometimes even sharing the same job (e.g. two people doing two and a half days each per week), working fewer and fewer hours, with periods of unemployment, and eventually, earlier retirement.

It's even becoming old-fashioned to talk about jobs! The experts now talk about 'work'. They say that although there may be a shortage of 'jobs', there's never a shortage of 'work' if you include different ways of working:

■ employment which is part-   ■ self-employment
   time or temporary   ■ volunteering

51

Interests	Examples
scientific	very interested in how and why things work
social	keen to help people in need
general	keen to provide a service to people
influencing	love organising, debating, advising
literary	enjoy using words, either writing or speaking
artistic	love creating or entertaining
computational	keen on working with figures or computers
practical	keen on making, fixing, or operating things
nature	love the countryside, sea, plants, animals
active	keen on the outdoors, adventure

Hopes	Examples
respect	want people to look up to you
company	want to work with others
helping	want to help the homeless, starving or elderly
money	usually dreaming of a Porsche, Caribbean holidays etc.
results	determined to achieve important things
power	want to make decisions that matter
satisfaction	couldn't do a job unless it was worthwhile
learning	want to go on learning new skills
variety	can't stand one place or one activity for too long
independence	don't want someone breathing down your neck
creating	very keen to create or entertain
security	don't want risks, especially to pay or prospects
lifestyle	don't want work to interfere with other activities

THE FUTURE

But what sort of work will there be in the future? The answer seems to be 'services'. Two out of every three workers now provide services (nursing, teaching, computing, hairdressing, driving, banking, typing, accounting, selling, travel, leisure), instead of making goods (ship, cars), or producing raw materials (coal, oil).

Personality	Examples
adventurous	excited by challenge and risk
cautious	wait and see what others do first
leader	don't mind decision-making and responsibility
follower	happy to let others make decisions for you
loner	do things better if you do them alone
team-type	keen to work in a group
talker	happy to do the talking
listener	listen to advice and other opinions
tough	able to take criticism
sensitive	easily upset by other people
radical	keen to do things differently
conforming	usually follow the rules
confident	never worry about making mistakes
nervous	not sure of your abilities
determined	usually fight back against problems
easy going	usually patient, and happy to give and take

Skills	Examples
Types	
survival	fit; good with people; able to read and write
practical	good at metalwork, typing, art, sport
academic	good at physics, history, economics, French
Levels	
basic	no GCSEs; Youth Training certificate
general	have or should get several GCSEs; RSA; City and Guilds
further	have or could get A levels or BTEC/SCOTVEC National
higher	may be able to get BTEC Higher National or degree

All this means that we will need:
- skills to do various jobs
- the skill of dealing with people (needed for most service jobs)
- skills to cope with more leisure time (including unemployment)

53

WORK

Interests	Examples
scientific	engineer, astronomer, mechanic, technician, doctor
social	youth worker, nurse, police officer, minister
general	secretary, shop assistant, postal worker, clerk
influencing	fashion buyer, solicitor, sales rep., designer, teacher
literary	journalist, librarian, teacher, translator, barrister
artistic	photographer, actor, beauty therapist, hairdresser
computational	wages clerk, accountant, programmer, cashier
practical	decorator, bricklayer, dressmaker, electrician
nature	farmer, vet, gardener, forester, shepherd, stablehand
active	soldier, jockey, sea fisherman, professional sportsperson

Hopes	Examples
respect	dentist, pilot, entertainer, technician
company	nanny, model, dancer, sales assistant
helping	speech therapist, social worker, ambulance driver
money	stockbroker, advertising executive, architect
results	builder, cook, designer, vet, carpenter, tailor
power	politician, police officer, town planner
satisfaction	blacksmith, youth worker, baker, historian
learning	armed forces, scientist, gardener, doctor
variety	sales rep., travel courier, journalist, actor
independence	gamekeeper, shopkeeper, accountant, farmer
creating	window-dresser, camera operator, musician
security	librarian, doctor, teacher, clerk, typist
lifestyle	factory assistant, farmer, youth worker

 CONTACTS

■ local careers officer   ■ school careers teacher

 READING

Here are just some of the books which you may be able to see at your local, school, college, careers office or Jobcentre library:

■ *Signposts Box* (Careers and Occupational Information Centre (COIC)): a green plastic box full of cards about many different jobs

■ *Working In . . .* booklets: about all sorts of work (COIC)

Personality	Examples
adventurous	seaman, travel courier, inventor, member of H.M. forces
cautious	clerk, accountant, librarian, refuse collector
leader	manager, chef, supervisor, soldier
follower	secretary, typist, shop assistant, clerk
loner	window-cleaner, sales rep., shepherd, driver
team-type	fire officer, stagehand, diver, nurse
talker	travel courier, entertainer, sales rep.
listener	social worker, solicitor, doctor, youth worker
tough	prison officer, armed forces, barrister
sensitive	bill poster, typist, gardener, dressmaker
radical	politician, solicitor, entertainer, union official
conforming	police officer, clerk, secretary, traffic warden
confident	doctor, sales rep., supervisor, pilot, manager
nervous	shepherd, typist, artist, gardener
determined	actor, journalist, sales rep., politician
easy going	playgroup worker, youth worker, minister

Skills	Examples
Types	
survival	cleaner, playgroup worker, traffic warden, seaman
practical	typist, mechanic, technician, farmer, hairdresser
academic	teacher, librarian, administrator, doctor
Levels	
basic	warehouse assistant, florist, porter, messenger
general	secretary, clerk, nurse, forester, beauty therapist
further	supervisor, chef, technician, programmer
higher	manager, architect, designer, scientist, teacher

- *Job Outlines . . .* booklets: about all sorts of work (COIC)
- *Unqualified Success:* really useful if you have no qualifications (Penguin)
- *Careers and Jobs without O Levels* (Careers Research and Advisory Centre (CRAC, Hobsons Press)
- *Employment For Disabled People* (Kogan Page)
- *Occupations* (COIC): there's a new one each year
- *Careers Encyclopedia* (Cassell)
- *The Job Book* (CRAC)
- *Equal Opportunities for Women and Men* (Penguin)

- *Job Ideas* (COIC)
- *Jobs In. . .* books: about all sorts of work (Kogan Page)
- *Careers In. . .* books: about all sorts of work (Kogan Page)
- newspaper and magazine articles, and radio and TV programmes about people and their jobs

CHOOSING ▶▶▶

ADVICE

Vital. Local careers officers and school careers teachers can give you the latest and best advice. It's also important to find out what a job is *really* like, from the people actually doing it. Ask the careers experts if they could arrange visits to or from employers. Also speak to relatives, friends and anybody you see doing a job that interests you.

RIGHT

The right choice of careers is the choice that's right for *you*. Although you need all the advice you can get, only *you* can make the right choice. It can be a disaster to allow yourself to be pushed into the wrong job by a careers officer, careers teacher, friend or parent. After all, you're the one who has to do all the work!

It can be just as bad to push yourself into the wrong career: for example, applying for the first job you see advertised. Above all, remember that you don't have to choose what 'everybody else' is doing, because there is no 'everybody else':
- there are men who are nurses, secretaries, playgroup workers, translators, house-husbands, dancers
- there are women who are lorry drivers, mechanics, managers, programmers
- there are black people who are police officers, newsreaders, council leaders.
- there are blind politicians, artists, broadcasters
- there are 16 year olds running their own businesses
and so on.

WHAT

It might help to use the two lists suggested already, to try and spot the best matches between your interests, skills, personality and hopes, and the careers that interest you. See page 50. It's well worth doing this several times over a few weeks, perhaps changing both lists several times as you think about yourself and about careers. You may even decide on two careers. But check your choice with a careers expert.

YOU AND WORK: MATCHING UP

	NURSE	BRICKLAYER	MANAGER	GARDENER (self-employed)
Interests scientific social nature	✓	✗	✗	✓
Skills Type practical Level basic	✗	✓	✗	✓
Personality adventurous tough determined	✓	✗	✓	✓
Hopes money satisfaction independence	?	✗	✓	✓

CAN'T?

Can't choose? Don't panic! You may not have to make a decision just yet, especially if you're still at school. Of course it won't help to put it all off and end up not bothering at all. That could mean years wasted drifting on the dole, or in the wrong job. Remember

■ *you can* keep your options open by taking a good mixture of courses

- *you can* get a job which would give you a clearer picture of work (e.g. work experience from school, volunteering, a Saturday job or a holiday job)

NEXT

You need to
- find out what skills (and experience or qualifications) you need for that career (from a careers expert)
- find out how to get the skills you need (see page 9)
- find the job! (see page 85)

READING

- free leaflets from local careers officers and school careers teachers
- *Decisions at 13/14+* (Careers Research and Advisory Centre (CRAC))
- *Decisions at 15/16+* (CRAC)
- *Decisions at 17/18+* (CRAC)

EMPLOYMENT

Working for someone else is the way most people work. There are a few things worth knowing that could help you to make a success of it.

W H Y ▶▶▶

Why work for someone else?

Good:
- employer pays your tax and National Insurance, gives you paid holidays, sick pay and maternity leave and so on.
- definitely paid
- security
- good way to get experience, even for self-employment

All addresses in Addresses!

59

Bad:
- have to do what you're told
- money may be OK, but probably not great
- may have to put up with difficult people at work

- may not be able to show what you can really do
- profit matters more than you do

and so on.

WHAT ▶▶▶

There's more to choosing employment than choosing careers.

SIZE

Small companies may offer more freedom, a chance to do different jobs, a chance to see a job through from start to finish, a friendlier atmosphere . . .

Large companies may offer better training, better prospects for promotion, higher wages, bonuses . . .

TIME

Full-time work (more than 16 hours a week) may offer better pay, job security, holiday pay, and plenty of rights (sick pay, redundancy money etc.)

Part-time or temporary work (one out of every four jobs) may be easier to get, give you plenty of free time (to run your own business, take college courses, look after children), help you to beat unemployment (could also lead to full-time work) and be a great opportunity to travel, get experience, or earn holiday money. But you may be overworked and underpaid, have less protection under the law, not be able to pay enough National Insurance Contributions (needed for some benefits), not get paid holidays, and have poor prospects of promotion.

OWNERSHIP

Public employers include British Rail, the National Health Service (NHS), the BBC and local government. Some have been bought (nationalised) from private employers (e.g. British Coal and British Rail). Public employers provide valuable public service, and may offer more job security.

Private employers include Marks & Spencer, ICI, Boots, and local offices and shops. Some larger ones have been sold (privatised) from public ownership (e.g. British Telecom and British Airways). You can buy a bit of (a share in) some companies (confusingly called Public Limited Companies e.g. Marks & Spencer PLC, and Imperial Chemical Industries PLC) on the Stock Exchange in London. When several people start a company, they may also own shares in it (a Limited Company, like Bloggs Ltd). There are also co-operatives, owned and run by their workers; partnerships, owned by 2–20 people; and sole traders. See page 73. Private employers may offer more challenge, more scope to show what you can do, and the chance of sharing in their ownership and decision-making.

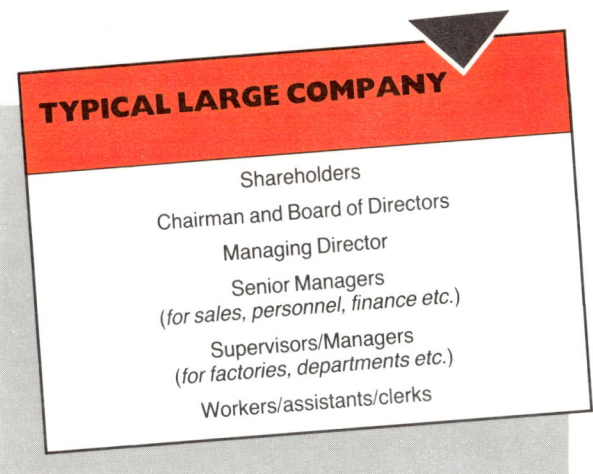

TYPICAL LARGE COMPANY

Shareholders

Chairman and Board of Directors

Managing Director

Senior Managers
(*for sales, personnel, finance etc.*)

Supervisors/Managers
(*for factories, departments etc.*)

Workers/assistants/clerks

S T A R T I N G ▶▶▶

Starting work should be a great new experience. You may be nervous, embarrassed and shy, just like other people, and you may come up against a few problems, just like other people. But, like most people, you'll probably settle into a new way of life before you know it.

You may be given a proper training (induction) course or simply 'shown the ropes'. Either way, it's well worth using this time to:

- learn how to use things: photocopier, duplicator, internal phone system, coffee machine etc.
- learn who does what (say hello, and they'll help you later on)
- learn where things are: lockers, toilets, fire exit, canteen, first aid box, recreation room etc.
- learn the basics of the job

and so on.

Remember that in many jobs all that really matters is:
- enthusiasm
- determination to work hard
- showing that you're keen to listen and learn
- arriving on time (shows respect for workmates, customers and employers)
- working as well as you can

and so on.

CONTRACT

You have one simply by being an employee. Things that were agreed at the interview are part of it. It doesn't have to be written down until you've worked for an employer for more than 16 hours a week and for more than 13 weeks. It's then called a 'written statement of terms and conditions of employment'. If you're not given one, or if it's not clear, get expert advice (see Contacts below) before you sign it.

WRITTEN CONTRACT

- date when you started
- how your pay is worked out
- hours of work
- holidays
- length of notice you must give before leaving
- what happens if you do something wrong
- how to complain
- any sick pay, pension schemes etc.
- how to get this information if it isn't in the contract

JOB DESCRIPTION

Your employer doesn't have to give you a description of your duties, but it's worth asking for one. If you do get one, but it's not clear, get expert advice before you sign it.

PAY

You'll be paid at the end of the each week or month. In other words, the employer always owes you money, which can be kept from you if you leave. without giving enough warning (notice). If you're broke before the first pay day, you may be able to claim benefits (see page 117), or ask for an advance of wages.

If you're on a low wage you may be able to claim benefits to help with your living and housing costs (see page 117).

Most employers will take Income Tax and National Insurance Contributions off your wages (see page 114).

If you work for more than 16 hours a week, you must be given a pay slip, every time you are paid. Mistakes do happen so it's worth checking your pay slips, and keeping them as proof that you've paid Income Tax, National Insurance etc.

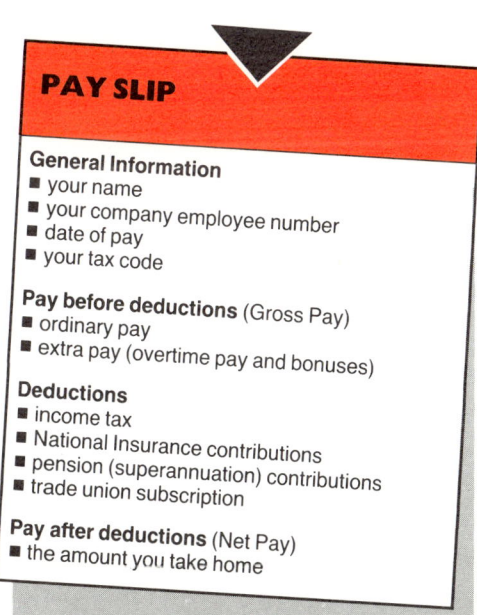

PAY SLIP

General Information
- your name
- your company employee number
- date of pay
- your tax code

Pay before deductions (Gross Pay)
- ordinary pay
- extra pay (overtime pay and bonuses)

Deductions
- income tax
- National Insurance contributions
- pension (superannuation) contributions
- trade union subscription

Pay after deductions (Net Pay)
- the amount you take home

DANGER

Often hidden: hanging chains, wet patches on the floor or open filing cabinet drawers; also germs, noise, vibration, sparks, dust, heat, fumes, dirt, radiation or chemicals which can take hours, days, weeks, months or even years to show their effects (poisoning, blindness, deafness, disease). Even sitting in front of a computer screen without regular breaks can give you headaches. It's vital to:

- ask for safety training
- wear all the right head/ear/eye/face/hand/foot/mouth protection: masks, goggles, helmets, mufflers, strong boots (not trainers), gloves, overalls etc.
- use safety guards on machines
- use the right tools and equipment for the job
- ask an expert how to use, clean, store, handle, prepare items such as food, chemicals or waste
- use the right methods of lifting, reaching, and carrying
- know where to find and how to use fire extinguishers, alarm buttons, fire exits, the first aid box etc.
- report anything that looks dangerous to your employer or trade union health and safety representative.

MUST

WEAR HELMET

WEAR EYE PROTECTION

MUSTN'T

SMOKE

USE NAKED FLAME

DANGER

FIRE

ELECTRIC SHOCK

FAWLTY TOWERS' KITCHEN

Health Inspector Mr Fawlty. . . these premises do not come up to the standard required by this authority;. . . specifically: lack of proper cleaning routines; dirty and greasy filters; greasy and encrusted deep fat frier; dirty, cracked and stained food preparation surfaces; dirty, cracked and missing wall and floor tiles; dirty, marked and stained utensils; dirty and greasy interior surfaces of the ventilator hoods; inadequate temperature control and storage of dangerous food stuffs; storage of cooked and raw meat in same trays; storage of raw meat above confectionery with consequent dripping of meat juices onto cream products; refrigerator seals loose and cracked; ice-box undefrosted and regrigerator over-stocked; food handling routines suspect; evidence of smoking in food preparation area; dirty and grubby food handling overalls . . . and 2 dead pigeons in the water tank.

Basil Fawlty Otherwise OK?

OPPORTUNITIES

The more you put into the job, the more you should get out of it
- it's well worth getting all the training you can, both inside and outside the organisation (see page 9). Ask your employer to consider paying your fees for a part-time college course (technology, crafts, shorthand, word processing, French, GCSEs etc.)
- there may be a company suggestions box, and prizes for good ideas
- there may be staff meetings where you can put forward your ideas
- there are young workers' exchanges abroad (see page 157)
- there is worthwhile trade union work to be done

UNION

Trade unions (such as the Transport and General Workers Union (TGWU) and the National Union of Public Employees

(NUPE)) are groups of workers organised to protect the jobs, pay, conditions, rights, safety and welfare of their members, and of workers around the world, whether full-time, part-time, temporary, trainees or unemployed. There are different unions for different sorts of work. You can choose whether or not you want to join a trade union, unless there's a 'closed shop', when you must join. You will have more power in a union than on your own. Some employers are very anti-union, so tread carefully. You can help to run/change a union by getting involved in meetings, elections, conferences, campaigns etc.

LEAVING

Could things get better if you stayed a big longer? If not, at least try to arrange another job before you leave. When leaving, a short and simple letter is best, giving the notice required under your contract. It's important not to say or do anything that could get you a bad leaving report (reference) which your next employer will want to see. A good reason to give would be: 'to develop my career', whether that's true or not!

CONTACT
- Trade Union Congress (TUC): if you don't have a trade union at work but still want to join a union

READING
- *Workfacts: For Young Workers* (Careers and Occupational Information Centre (COIC))
- free leaflet on safety from your employer or local careers office

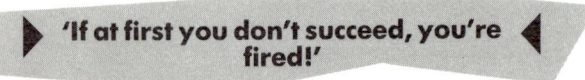

▶ 'If at first you don't succeed, you're fired!' ◀

H E L P ▶▶▶

Employees and employers have rights and responsibilities under the law. Employees must stick to agreements, work well, co-operate and be trustworthy. Employers must stick to agreements, mustn't ask employees to do anything illegal, and must look after employees' health and safety at work.

If you're under 18, or work less than 16 hours a week, you have fewer rights, but not so few that you should allow yourself to be pushed around.

SICK

Let your employer know immediately. If you are off sick for at least four days in a row, you should be able to get:
- Statutory Sick Pay from your employer for up to 28 weeks, if you earn over a certain (low) amount, or
- Sickness Benefit from the DHSS for up to 28 weeks, if you can't get Statutory Sick Pay, and if you've paid enough National Insurance Contributions, or
- Invalidity Benefit from the DHSS if you still can't work after 28 weeks, or
- Income Support from the DHSS
- see page 117

PREGNANT

Let your employer know immediately. You should be able to get:
- paid time off from your employer to see a doctor or go to a clinic, and
- time off (maternity leave) to have your baby, and your job back at the end of it, if you have worked for your employer at least 16 hours a week for at least two years, and
- Statutory Maternity Pay from your employer for up to 18 weeks, if you've been paying Class 1 National Insurance Contributions, and have worked for your employer for at least six months up to the 26th week of pregnancy, or
- Maternity Allowance from the DHSS for up to 18 weeks, if you can't get Statutory Maternity Pay, and if you've been paying National Insurance Contributions
- Maternity Payment: from the DHSS if you get Income Support or Family Credit.
- see page 117

ACCIDENT

Make sure it's written down in the Accident Book. Ask an expert (see Contacts) whether you can claim money (compensation). Claim benefits if you have to miss or leave work (see page 117).

HARASSMENT

If you have trouble with anyone at work because of your sex (sexual harassment), or race (racial harassment) take action or things could get worse. Speaking to the person bothering you could be the simplest and best answer. But if that doesn't work get others at work on your side and take action together, or contact a sympathetic trade union official, or a Citizens Advice Bureau.

UNFAIR

No matter what your sex or race you have a right to fair treatment over promotion, training, duties, conditions, rules, redundancy and so on. You should also take action about unfair treatment for other reasons such as pregnancy or trade union membership.

SACKED

For something as bad as stealing you can be sacked immediately. For offences such as causing trouble, being rude, always off work or always late you should get a warning first, and then about a week's notice. But if you think you've been sacked unfairly and if you've worked for your employer for at least a year and for more than 16 hours a week, you may be able to take your employer to an Industrial Tribunal to get compensation.

REDUNDANT

If you have to leave or are offered a poorer job because your employer is reorganising, closing down, or moving, and if you have worked for the employer for at least two years, for more than 16 hours a week, you may be able to get time off to look for work and at least half a week's pay for each year with the employer (redundancy money).

ACTION

Quick action can prevent a small problem becoming a big problem
- having a chat with workmates, parents, a supervisor, a personnel officer, a careers officer, or your employer

68

- getting together with other people at work e.g. on a staff association
- getting help from a trade union shop steward or representative
- using the law (see page 169), e.g. taking your employer to an Industrial Tribunal to get compensation (only as a last resort though)

CONTACTS

- Citizens Advice Bureau
- careers officer (it doesn't matter that you've started work)
- local Law Centre
- local Department of Employment/ Unemployment Benefit Office: all sorts of information
- local Jobcentre

READING

- *Workfacts: For Young Workers* (Careers and Occupational Information Centre (COIC))
- free leaflets from your local Department of Employment/ Unemployment Benefit Office, or Department of Health and Social Security (DHSS) Office: on contracts, sick pay, unfair treatment, pregnancy, redundancy etc.

SELF~EMPLOYMENT

You CAN work for yourself. But will you and your business survive? It's tough, *very* tough. Many new businesses fail; and that's just one of the hard realities behind the dream.

But if you're the right sort of person, with the right idea, and the right plans, you could succeed in what some people find the most exciting, satisfying and best paid work of all.

All addresses in Addresses!

Why work for yourself?

Good:
- a job immediately (beating unemployment)
- independence
- freedom
- enthusiasm and determination may be more important than skills, experience or qualifications
- control over your work, and life
- if successful, the harder you work, the more you earn
- a way of expressing yourself
- may be able to work from home (also useful if you're disabled or have young children)

Bad:
- no sales, no meals
- have to boss yourself even more than an ordinary boss would!
- could be lonely
- some say the 'freedom' is a bit of a con, because you can end up being a slave to banks, worry, pressure, hard work . . .
- no paid holidays or sick leave
- may have to be ruthless: for example getting rid of your employees if you can't afford to pay them
- risk of losing money
- even more difficult when you're young and inexperienced (if you're under 18, your parents have to sign contracts for you)
- not only do you have to do the work, but also you have to find it first!

You are the most important part of your business. You don't have to be JR in *Dallas* or Alexis in *Dynasty*, but that would help.

PERSONALITY

Could you cope if you were lonely, broke, exhausted, bored, cheated, in debt? Are you adventurous, tough, enthusiastic, determined, confident? Many of our top business people have succeeded only after several big failures, but they had the right personality to bounce back.

SKILLS

You need skills to make goods or provide services, and skills to sell them. There are all sorts of opportunities (see page 9) to learn whatever skills you need, including signwriting, floristry, plumbing, and business skills of selling, managing, planning, book-keeping etc.

> ▶ 'When I do business I give them my ◀
> hand and my heart. Obviously
> they'd rather have a receipt and a
> guarantee, but you can't have
> everything, can you?'
> (Arthur Daley)

I D E A S ▶▶▶

You may have an idea, but do you have a good *business* idea? Will people buy it? Is it cheap/fast/stylish/reliable enough to beat the competition? Sure? Think of all those boutiques and small shops that come and go every five minutes. If you have to guess whether it's a business idea, *stop*! You need to test your ideas first by market research (asking people!) You can't do enough of it. Remember to ask strangers, not friends or relatives who might say 'yes' just to please you. You need to know:
■ will they buy it?
■ will they buy it at your price?
■ will they buy it from where you are selling it?
■ how often will they buy it?

It's not what you do, it's the way that you do it. Success takes imagination, nerve, style ... Simple and cheap ideas are often best. Many people laugh at the idea of being a window cleaner, but a window cleaner needs nothing more than a bucket, 'shammy' leather, wiper-blade, detergent, ladder, and insurance. Starting costs could be under £100. By choosing an expensive area to clean windows, you could make a lot of money very quickly, with few expenses or worries, while other businesses are struggling with rent, rates, loans, equipment costs etc. Then who would be laughing?

IDEAS

Services
(often cheaper to set up)
cleaning (cars, windows, chimneys . .)
signwriting
gardening
mobile disco
hairdressing
journalism
decorating
taxi
computer programming
photography/video filming
sandwiches (e.g. taking round offices)
removals
typing
knitting
bicycle repair
gardening
messenger service

Goods

earrings
candlesticks
inventions!
stamps
computer software
health foods
fishing tackle
local magazine
games
pottery
furniture
flowers
junk
fashion clothes
stained glass

PLANS ▶▶▶

The experts say, plan, plan, plan, and plan again. You need to show these plans to people you approach for help.

TYPE

There are big differences between various types of business.

- Sole trader: on your own
  Good: no hassle from partners; very easy to set up
  Bad: lonely; fully responsible for your debts
- Partnership: 2–20 people
  Good: not so lonely; sharing responsibility for debts
  Bad: many partners fall out (so get a partnership agreement from a solicitor)
- Limited Company: several people share the ownership (as shareholders)
  Good: you're not responsible for company debts
  Bad: costly to set up (you need proper legal documents)

- Co-operative: everyone shares in ownership, decision-making, work, profits, losses etc. and may be paid the same wage
  Good: spirit of sharing
  Bad: co-operative theory *v.* capitalist practice (e.g. it's not easy to make hard business decisions at general meetings)
- Freelance: you provide a service such as photography, hairdressing, journalism, computer programming, or graphic design
  Good: control over work you enjoy
  Bad: you're paid only for each piece of work you do, so you need a steady stream of work; may not be possible if you already work as an employee (i.e. breaking contract)
- Commission: selling things for other people (insurance, double-glazing, office equipment etc.)
  Good: easy to get
  Bad: could be a dodgy firm; may lose money on travelling expenses; product or service may be difficult to sell
- Homeworker: work brought to you by someone else (addressing envelopes, typing, knitting)
  Good: working at home
  Bad: low pay; lonely

MONEY

Costs

Even a roaring trade doesn't mean success if you have too many costs to knock off your sales income:

- materials
- a *realistic* wage for yourself
- wages for any employees
- repayment of loans
- loan interest
- rent
- rates
- National Insurance contributions
- income tax
- heating
- phone rental and calls
- postage
- delivery
- advertising
- lighting
- petrol
- insurance
and so on.

74

Saving

But it is possible to cut your starting costs:
- using your bedroom or a market stall or a low cost start-up unit from the council or sharing premises with others
- hiring equipment
- getting your supplies on credit (with a month or so before you have to pay for them)

and so on.

Funds

- savings from a job: no loan to repay, no security needed, no worry and no fuss
- loan from relatives: low or no interest and no need to offer security; but mixing relationships and money can lead to trouble
- loan from a youth enterprise scheme: cheap (low interest) loan, maybe up to five years to pay it back, and they understand your problems and will help you
- bank loan (see page 113): if you are turned down by several bank managers, try several more (some understand your problems, others haven't got a clue)
- Enterprise Allowance: if you're at least 18, you (and any partners) can get a regular cheque from the government (£40 a week in 1988) to help with your expenses in the first year. First you must have £1000, but this could be a loan or promise of a loan from a bank, youth enterprise agency, relative ... Wait until you're sure of your idea though, otherwise you could waste the Enterprise Allowance on a dud idea
- benefits (see page 117)

Plans

Many business fail, not because they lack sales, or sales income, but because they don't have enough hard cash coming in quickly enough to pay the bills. All seems to be going well and suddenly they run out of money. So one of the most important plans is a Cash Flow Forecast. That's a fancy name for a calculation of weeks and months when you're likely to be short of money. If you show it to your bank manager you may get permission to become overdrawn at these times (see page 113).

CONTROL

It's vital to keep clear, accurate and up-to-date records (including all receipts) and a separate business bank account, so that you can:
- keep control of your business and check on its health
- add up your business expenses (heating, stamps, petrol, loan interest, accountant's fees etc.) to be knocked off your tax bill (see page 114)
- avoid a mix up between personal and business money

and so on.

REGULATIONS

Red tape is a headache, but it can't be avoided. You have to:
- pay your own (and any employees') income tax and National Insurance contributions (see page 114)
- get a special licence from the local council for certain types of business (e.g. selling food)
- get permission from your local council Planning Department (e.g. if you're working from home)
- obey employment laws if you employ people (see page 66)
- get special insurance for premises, contents, stock, employees, customers, etc.

HELP ▶▶▶

Instead of wasting time and money on a dud idea, it makes sense to get as much information, advice and help as possible when starting and running your business. A lot of it is free.

YOUTH ENTERPRISE SCHEMES

Many have local branches, others can put you in touch with useful local contacts.

ENTERPRISE AGENCIES

Local, national and UK agencies; some have a youth enterprise section; they can also put you in touch with useful local contacts.

PROFESSIONALS

- bank manager: loans, insurance
- accountant: tax, financial records
- solicitor: contracts, property, licences

CONTACTS

- *Youth Enterprise Schemes:*
  Youth Business Trust (Prince's Trust)
  Livewire (also awards prizes for good business ideas)
  Project Fullemploy Ltd
  Young Enterprise (including help to set up a *real* business at
  school)
  Practical Action
  Instant Muscle
  Youth Enterprise Scheme
- *Enterprise Agencies*
  UK: Small Firms Service
  Scotland: Scottish Development Agency (SDA)
  Wales: Welsh Development Agency (WDA)
  Northern Ireland: Local Enterprise Development Agency
  (LEDU)
  Council for Small Industries in Rural Areas (COSIRA)
  Cooperative Development Agency (CDA)
- *Also*
  local careers officer
  Jobcentre (Jobmarket in Northern Ireland): information about
  the Enterprise Allowance Scheme and the Training for
  Enterprise Scheme (a course for anyone starting a business)
  your local council: information, advice and help

READING

- *Working In . . . Self Employment* (Careers & Occupational
  Information Centre (COIC))
- *Job Outlines: Self Employment* (COIC)
- *Your Own Business* (Careers Research and Advisory Centre
  (CRAC))
- *Work for Yourself: A Guide For Young People* (National
  Extension College (NEC))
- *Be Your Own Boss At 16* (Kogan Page)
- *Self-Sufficiency 16–25* (Kogan Page)
- *Co-operating for Work* (COIC): partnerships and co-
  operatives

VOLUNTEERING

W H Y
W H A T
W H E R E

There are people who need your help right now. The reward could be much greater than money. And voluntary work is about helping yourself too.

W H Y ▶▶▶

Good:
- helping others
- important work that won't be done if you don't do it
- a job immediately (beating unemployment)
- great way to fill spare time
- enthusiasm is all you need (though for a few jobs, especially overseas, you need skills that you can teach others)
- opportunities for all ages (though for many jobs you have to be at least 16, or 18, or 21)
- a chance to do things you've never done before and may never get a chance to do again
- a chance to travel and learn about other people's histories, cultures, living conditions . . .

78

All addresses in Addresses!

- learning skills (dealing with people, building, gardening . . .)
- expenses paid (travel, clothes, meals, equipment, bed . . .)
- may be able to claim benefits (see pages 80 and 122)
- could lead to employment or self-employment through the people you meet and the skills you learn
and so on.

Bad:
- little or no pay
- could be learning skills at college
- not a career
- people will be relying on you so you must turn up
and so on.

> ▶ **'I joined the army for three reasons.** ◀
> **First, I wanted to defend my country.**
> **Second, I knew it would make a man**
> **of me. Third, they sent two big**
> **blokes in red caps to get me.'**
> **(Eric Morecambe)**

WHAT ▶▶▶

The list of things is almost endless, because the list of things that need to be done is almost endless:
- building adventure playgrounds
- repairing community buildings
- shopping for the elderly
- taking disabled people to soccer matches
- being a disc jockey on hospital radio
- helping in a night shelter for the homeless
- building schools, roads, houses, canals, drains . . .
- teaching English, farming, nursing, bricklaying . . .
- protecting plant and animal life
- helping on an archaeological dig
- working in a charity office
- helping in a home for physically or mentally disabled people
and so on.

WHERE ▶▶▶

Everywhere: from next door, to Africa!

〰 *CONTACTS*

Local:
- careers officer (see page 7)
- local Volunteer Bureau or local Council for Voluntary Service (address from library or phone book)
- local Jobcentre (Jobmarket in Northern Ireland): if you're at least 16 ask about the Voluntary Projects Programme (in Northern Ireland, the Community Volunteering Scheme) which allows you to volunteer without losing benefits
- Community Service Volunteers (CSV): all sorts of opportunities if you're at least 16 (they don't turn anyone away)
- Citizens Advice Bureau
- local youth workers

UK:
- Community Service Volunteers (CSV): if you're at least 16; endless list of opportunities from 4 to 12 months
- British Trust for Conservation Volunteers (BTCV): two week projects
- International Voluntary Service (IVS): ask about workcamps
- Royal Association for Disability and Rehabilitation (RADAR): information for both able-bodied and disabled people who are at least 16
- Young Volunteer Bureau of the National Youth Bureau (NYB)

Overseas:
- International Voluntary Service (IVS): if you're at least 18; opportunities abroad, including workcamps, for at least two weeks
- Voluntary Service Overseas (VSO): if you're at least 18; usually they need volunteers with skills, for about two years
- British Volunteer Programme

〰 *READING*

Local:
- newspaper ads
- Yellow Pages (under 'Voluntary')

UK:
- *Voluntary Organisations* (National Council for Voluntary Organisations;
- *Youth Action Address List* (free from Young Volunteer Bureau of the National Youth Bureau (NYB))

Overseas:
- *Volunteer Work Abroad* (Central Bureau for Educational Visits and Exchanges (CBEVE))
- *International Directory of Voluntary Work* (Vacation Work Publications (VWP))

UNEMPLOYMENT

Beat it. Use it. It's not your fault. Remember that you're not alone: millions of people are unemployed.

You can replace many of the things you get from work (page 50) in other ways.

And don't worry; what matters is not that you were unemployed, but what you did while you were unemployed.

ACTION ▶▶▶

Lying in bed, hanging round the streets and afternoons of TV are bound to get you down. Why let that happen? There's so much to do! There are many ideas in the chapters of this book.

SECRETS

■ choosing better *options*/
   subjects to learn

■ budgeting your *money*
■ claiming *benefits*

82

*All addresses
in Addresses!*

- taking advantage of *opportunities* to get skills
- learning some of the *basics* such as using computers
- choosing the right *career* to aim for
- applying for part-time or temporary *employment*
- trying *self-employment*
- *volunteering* for work experience
- *job-finding;* it's a full time job
- making *decisions* for a better future
- learning *survival* skills to stay fit in body and mind
- learning to handle *relationships*
- finding a *home* nearer to jobs
- getting *help* to sort out any problems
- finding out *what's on*, so that you're not cut off.
- making the most out of cheap *travel* to get away from it all
- finding out about the *law* and your rights
- taking *action* to get a better deal for unemployed people

 ## READING

- *The New Unemployment Handbook* (National Extension College (NEC))
- *Facing Unemployment* (Careers Research and Advisory Centre (CRAC))
- *How to Survive Unemployment* (Penguin)

> ▶ **'I don't know what we'd do without you. But we're going to try.'** ◀

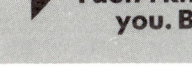 **C E N T R E** ▶▶▶

Unemployment centres have different names: centres for the unemployed, drop-in centres, YMCA centres, unemployed projects, TUC centres ... but they all offer at least some of these things:
- a chance to meet people in the same boat
- snooker, table-tennis, five-a-side soccer, drama workshops ...
- cheap snacks
- a chance to learn about, and use, video, photographic, music, printing and computer equipment
- a chance to learn survival skills (writing, job-finding, cooking, arithmetic, form-filling, letter-writing, staying fit ...)

- information about benefits, what's on, cheap travel etc.
- a chance to chat to youth workers about any problem and so on.

⚋ CONTACTS

- your local library: address of the nearest unemployment centre

JOB~FINDING

Jobs don't go to the best or cleverest people; they go to those who are best organised and most determined to get them.

And finding work is a full-time job!

READY? ▶▶▶

SKILLS

Have you checked out all the opportunities to pick up some skills, experience and qualifications first? You could have some fun now, and get a better job later.

CAREERS

You can save time chasing after the wrong jobs by carefully choosing the right career (see page 49).

All addresses in Addresses!

85

PERSONAL INFORMATION SHEET

Sometimes called a curriculum vitae or cv (Latin for 'course of life'), listing your education, interests, any work experience etc. You can photocopy it, send a copy with each job application letter, and give a copy to each job interviewer, to make sure you get across all the important information about yourself (even if you're nervous). It should be:

- on unlined, white A4 size paper (210 × 297mm)
- clear, neat, and brief (one side of the page only)
- typed
- honest: you may be asked about anything you write
- full of interesting things about you (don't worry if you haven't got qualifications: mention hobbies, sports, interests . . .)

JOB-FINDING TIMETABLE

When	Where/What
8.30– 9.30	Home answering mail
9.30–10.45	Jobcentre, careers office, local library reading latest ads writing about jobs
10.45–12.15	Employers visiting/phoning
12.15–12.30	Post office posting letters first class
12.30– 2.00	Unemployment centre lunch chat pool, darts . . . drama, photography, video, cookery . . . going to a talk about benefits, housing . . .
2.00– 3.00	College of further education typing/computer/French/arithmetic course
3.00– 5.00	Jobcentre, careers office, local library reading latest ads writing/phoning about jobs
5.00– 5.15	Post office posting letters first class
5.15– 6.15	Leisure centre swimming, weight-training, table tennis . . .

REFEREES

Employers will want to contact two people who know you and your school, training, college, or work record. That means teachers, headteachers, supervisors, lecturers, employers or youth workers, but not friends or relatives. At this stage you need only ask if they'll give you a reference when you need one. You won't see the reference, so make sure you can trust your referees to say something helpful.

JOB-FINDING KIT

- cheap cardboard folders for letters, forms, certificates
- a note book to list addresses, dates of letters sent and received, people contacted, etc.
- a supply of white, unlined, A4 sized paper
- a supply of long white or brown envelopes
- a highlighter pen
- bus and train timetables
- street map from a local estate agent or local tourist office
- stamps

PEACE

You can get peace, and a desk to write letters, in the reference section of your local library, or at a Job Club (see page 89).

JOB-FINDING SKILLS

You can get help to write letters, prepare a Personal Information Sheet, fill in application forms, etc. from the Contacts below.

CONTACTS

- local careers officer (see page 7)
- school careers teacher
- local Jobcentre/Jobmarket
- Apex Trust: if you've been in trouble with the law
- local printing shops/ workshops: cheap paper and envelopes

READING

- *Job Hunting Kit* (Careers and Occupational Information Centre (COIC))

- *My Job Application File* (Careers Research and Advice Centre (CRAC))
- *Job Hunter Kit* (Apex Trust): if you've been in trouble with the law
- *Wiping the Slate Clean* (free leaflet from a Citizens Advice Bureau): if you've been in trouble with the law

LOOKING ▶▶▶

Everywhere, everyday. New jobs are advertised every day, sometimes in the last places you'd expect to see ads.

ADVERTS

Careful! 'Rodent Engineer' *does* mean rat-catcher! Try to spot the bad jobs and bad employers before wasting time on them. If an ad doesn't promise you a fortune, and is sensibly written, it's probably OK. If they say they want a genius, that means you.

ADS

ess.	essential
exp.	experience (the dreaded word)
HGV	Heavy Goods Vehicle (e.g. lorry) driving licence
negotiable	to be agreed with you
p.a.	per annum/year, or personal assistant
perm.	permanent
p.m.	per month
pref.	preferred (not essential)
PSV	Public Service Vehicle (e.g. bus) driving licence
p.t.	part-time
p.w.	per week
sae	stamped addressed envelope (see page 32)
reqd.	required
self emp.	self-employed
temp.	temporary worker (e.g. temporary typist)
w/p	word processing
wpm	words per minute (typing speed)

CAREERS OFFICER AND CAREERS TEACHER

As well as telling you about careers, and special ways of applying for special careers (e.g. armed forces), they can tell you about some of the latest job vacancies. See page 7.

JOBCENTRE

Jobmarket in Northern Ireland. If you're disabled, ask to see a Disablement Resettlement Officer (DRO). A goldmine of information about jobs and training schemes. There's a self-service system: jobs are described on postcards displayed on racks. If you want to know more about a job, make a note of its reference number and give the number to the person at the desk. They may be able to fix up an interview within the hour (so go to the Jobcentre dressed for an interview). There's also a Job Library full of useful reading. Ask about the:
- Youth Training (see page 14)
- Community Industry Scheme (in some large cities and towns)
- Voluntary Projects Programme (see page 80)
- Job Training Scheme
- Community Programme: if you're at least 18, and have been unemployed for six months, there are jobs open to you only. They last for a year, and the pay is usually OK.
- Job-Start Allowance: if you're at least 18, and have been unemployed for more than a year, and take a full-time job with wages of less than £80 a week you may be able to get £20 a week extra for six months.
- Job Club: if you're at least 18, and have been unemployed for at least six months, you can join a group of fellow job-hunters and have the free use of a desk, phone, typewriter, paper, pens, envelopes, stamps, directories, and a photocopier; a free read of newspapers and magazines; and free advice and help to prepare a Personal Information Sheet, write letters, fill in application forms etc.
- Training for Enterprise Scheme (a course to help you set up your own bussiness)

NEWSPAPERS AND MAGAZINES

Read them as soon as they come out. You can see them for nothing at your local library or Jobcentre. Also take a look at trade journals such as *Nursing Times*, and *Travel Trade Gazette*.

EMPLOYERS

Some employers don't advertise vacancies, or don't advertise them very well. You can visit, phone or write to any employer (see Yellow Pages) and ask if they have any 'vacancies' or 'opportunities' (sounds better than 'jobs'). It's best to contact an owner, manager, personnel manager, or foreman and use his/her name (which you can get from the phone switchboard). At the very least, leave your Personal Information Sheet. Remind them that they may be able to get a grant through the local Jobcentre/Jobmarket to employ you (e.g. under the Youth Training or New Workers schemes). Also listen for news of organisations setting up in your area, and write to their head office (address from a careers officer).

GRAPEVINE

Sometimes it may be *who* you know, rather than what you know that gets you the job. Family, friends, youth leaders, secretaries, caretakers or cleaners may hear of job vacancies.

ADVERTISING

A short and snappy ad in a local paper or shop window can produce excellent results.

RADIO

Many local radio stations broadcast news of job vacancies throughout the day.

NOTICES

Outside factories, shops, offices ...

VOLUNTEERING

You could meet people who could tell you about, or even give you, a job. See page 78.

AGENCIES

Private companies such as Alfred Marks Bureau and Brook Street Bureau. Unfortunately they're not much use unless you are at least 18 and have skills such as typing, book keeping or accounting. They may interview you and keep your name on file in case an organisation is looking for somebody with your skills, or they may employ you and send you out to other organisations e.g. to do secretarial 'temping'.

AWAY FROM HOME

Cities and the south-east of England may have more jobs, but if you're young, unskilled, inexperienced and unqualified, your chances may be much the same as at home. Finding a new place to live is also a big problem (see page 134). Ask your Jobcentre for information, advice and help.

ABROAD

You need your parents' permission if you're under 18, and you need a work-permit from the country's London embassy, unless it's an EC country (Belgium, Denmark, France, Greece, Holland, Ireland, Italy, Luxembourg, Portugal, Spain or West Germany). Unfortunately they may not give you one, because you'd be taking a job from their own people. But see page 157.

> ▶ 'It's not what you know, it's who you ◀
> know, isn't it?'
> 'Yeah, trouble is, I don't know either
> of them.'

A P P L Y I N G ▶▶▶

The secret is to be the person they're looking for:
- enthusiastic
- friendly
- keen to listen and learn
- efficient
- polite
- with a spark of life and initiative

and so on.

That means:
- replying to ads and letters immediately
- presenting yourself well: voice, dress, handwriting …
- mentioning any Saturday jobs, hobbies, sports, voluntary work, evening classes, travel …
- taking the trouble (unlike the other candidates) to find out something about the organisation and its products or

services, by writing for a company brochure, and asking your careers teacher or careers officer and so on.

Writing about a job

THISTLE MATTRESSES LTD

Always up to scratch

303, Itchyback Road, Dundee, DD1 1UD.

We require an enthusiastic and hard working school leaver to train as a warehouse assistant in our Dundee factory.

Reply to: Mr V. Ruff-Knight,
Personnel Manager

Mr V. Ruff-Knight
Personnel Manager
Thistle Mattresses Ltd.,
303, Itchyback Road,
Dundee
DD1 1UD

34, Dundreamin Avenue
Perth
PH2 8HE

10th June 1988

Dear Sir,

I am replying to your advertisement in today's Highland Courier for a school leaver to train as a warehouse assistant.

I shall be leaving Gorse Academy this month, after taking Standard Grade exams in English and Mathematics. I have work experience with Auld and Rustie Tools in Perth where my responsibilities included receiving and inspecting stock. I enjoy being busy, working with other people, and dealing with customers. Above all, I am very keen to learn.

I would be grateful for an application form and further information about the company training scheme.

I am available for interview at any time from 21st June.

Please find enclosed a Personal Information Sheet.

Yours faithfully

James Brown

JAMES BROWN

Phoning about a job

> **FLASH ENTERPRISES LTD**
> Second Hand Cars
> *Our word is your guarantee*
>
> We require a trainee car sales assistant. Please phone Mr McCann, Personnel Officer, on 01-345 7891

Switchboard	Flash Enterprises. Good morning. Can I help you?
Michelle	Good morning. My name is Michelle Stewart. I would like to speak to Mr McCann, the Personnel Officer, about the vacancy for a trainee car sales assistant advertised in this morning's *Fulham Bugle*.
Switchboard	One moment please.
Mr McCann	Good morning, Terence McCann speaking.
Michelle	Good morning Mr McCann. My name is Michelle Stewart. I am phoning about the vacancy for a trainee car sales assistant advertised in this morning's *Fulham Bugle*.
Mr McCann	Ah yes, we've had quite a few enquiries already. Could you give me some details about yourself?
Michelle	*(She has her Personal Information Sheet beside her, as a reminder.)* Yes certainly. I am 17 and I left Hardgrind College in Balham at the end of June. I have 3 GCSEs: English, Maths and French, and I'm taking an evening class in Information Technology. Last year I had a Saturday job in a DIY store, and at the moment I am doing voluntary work in a shelter for homeless people.
Mr McCann	Well that seems OK. Now would you like me to send you an application form?
Michelle	Yes please.
Mr McCann	I'll need your full address please. *(Michelle says her address clearly and slowly to let him write it all down)*

Mr McCann	Fine. Well I look forward to receiving your application form, Michelle. I'll write to you when I've had a chance to go through all the applications.
Michelle	Thank you very much, Mr McCann.
Mr McCann	Goodbye.
Michelle	Goodbye.

INTERVIEWS

Forget the word 'interview'. It should be a meeting. The employer should get to know you, and you should get to know the employer, in a discussion. That's important. There are bad applicants and bad employers. You don't want to waste several years of your life in a bad job, or second-rate training. The secrets are:

■ prepare answers to simple questions about your school work, interests, ambitions etc., and to tricky questions such as: why you want to work for the organisation; what you think you could bring to the job; how you would deal with difficult customer;

■ prepare a couple of your own short but tough questions about training and prospects (not about pay and holidays)

■ the night before: set two alarm clocks; plan the journey so that you arrive at least half an hour early; get shoes and clothes ready; collect enough money for a taxi, in case the bus is delayed; collect together exam certificates; a pen, pencil, rubber and note pad (in case there's a simple English or arithmetic test) and the letter inviting you to the interview or the introduction card from the Jobcentre.

■ remember the obvious things to do, such as dressing neatly, and obvious things not to do, such as chewing gum or smoking

■ remember the less obvious things that are just as important: a good start (a smile and a cheerful 'good morning/afternoon'); a firm and confident handshake (but only if the interviewer offers first); looking at the interviewer's eyes all the time; and using the interviewer's name at the start and end of the interview

■ avoid simple 'yes' or 'no' answers, or droning on in reply to a simple question

■ if you admit you don't know or don't understand something, your honesty will impress

94

Job Application Form

CRAZY BARGAINS LTD   STAFF APPLICATION FORM   CONFIDENTIAL

POSITION: *Trainee Sales Assistant*

SURNAME: *PATEL* (Mr/Mrs/**Miss**)

FORENAME(S): *NIRMALA*

ADDRESS: *34a Rhondda Bend*
Swansea
SA1 5AP   TEL. NO: *None*

DATE OF BIRTH: *23/12/72*   PLACE OF BIRTH: *Llanelly*

NATIONALITY: *British*   MARITAL STATUS: *Single*

HEALTH
Please give details of any disability
NONE

EDUCATION

Name and address of school and colleges	Dates	Examinations	Dates	Grades
Toughslog School, Highpass Road, Swansea, SA4 5TR	*1989*	*AEB Basic Test Arithmetic*	*11.88*	*Merit*
		GCSE English	*6.89*	*waiting*
		GCSE Biology	*6.89*	*for result*

EMPLOYMENT

Name and address of employer	Position held	Date	Reason for leaving
None			

ADDITIONAL INFORMATION
Please give details of skills, interests, activities, sports . . .
Certificates for first aid and swimming   Learning how to sail
Youth-hostelling in Devon last summer   Keen interest in photography

REFEREES
Please give the names of 2 referees

Mr. H.R.D. Taskmaster
Principal
Toughslog School
Highpass Road
Swansea SA4 5TR

Rev. S.T. David,
The Manse
Spire Lane
Swansea
SA5 6VS

SIGNATURE *Nirmala Patel*   DATE *23/7/89*

- show that you're enthusiastic after the interview too, by asking when you'll hear the result; thanking the interviewer; and saying you're very interested in the job

and so on.

REJECTED?

You're not the only one. It happens to many people many times. You may be just one excellent applicant out of many excellent applicants. Most have to be unlucky. Your luck will change, as long as you keep matching yourself (your interests, skills, personality and hopes) to jobs that are right for you (see page 57).

Good luck.

READING

- *Coping With Interviews* (New Opportunity Press)

The problem with freedom is that you have to make decisions: about training, careers, health, money, relationships, politics ... Simply following the crowd isn't much help, because they can all be wrong!

Perhaps it's *how* decisions are made that makes them easy or difficult.

WHY ▶▶▶

Why bother to learn the skill of decision-making? Some people say that the best way to learn is from your mistakes. The man who started the huge IBM computer company once said that 'the way to succeed is to double your failure rate'!

But some mistakes can have serious consequences: poor training, the wrong qualifications, a job which you hate, business failure, accidents, lung cancer, unwanted pregnancy, jail ... So making decisions can't be left to the toss of a coin, or a last-minute panic.

One expert has said that the best decision-maker is like a top sports player who makes all the important decisions off the field; often the game is won or lost before it has begun.

TOUGH? ▶▶▶

No confidence? Can't decide on anything? Failed too many times? Afraid of sticking your neck out?

SECRETS

- getting expert advice
- gaining confidence from knowing that you've done your best to make a good decision
- standing up for what *you* think is right, no matter what others say or do, and despite all the difficulties
- looking at 'failure' as a beginning (experience), not an end

and so on.

YOU ▶▶▶

What's important? What's right/wrong? That's up to you. Or is it?

IMPORTANT?

- exams
- happiness
- career
- health
- honesty
- faith

- justice
- money
- freedom
- caring
- family

and so on.

RIGHT/WRONG?

- abortion
- free health care

- distribution of the world's wealth

98

- gambling
- private education
- socialism
- living together before marriage

- claiming benefits
- nuclear weapons
- swearing

and so on.

INFLUENCES?

- moods
- parents
- religious leaders
- friends
- adverts
- pop stars

- books
- local community
- videos
- teachers
- newspapers, magazines, radio and TV

and so on.

READING

There are books about the various beliefs (about what is important, and what is right/wrong) by which people choose to live their lives (both religious and non-religious), such as:
- *Religious Studies Made Simple* (Heinneman)
- *What Christians believe* (Lion)

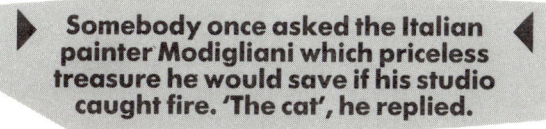

Somebody once asked the Italian painter Modigliani which priceless treasure he would save if his studio caught fire. 'The cat', he replied.

CHOICES ▶▶▶

Freedom to choose isn't much use without facts. Armed with facts about courses, careers, health, relationships and law, it's easier to see some *alternative* choices, and the *consequences* of making each choice.

CHOOSING ▶▶▶

ADVICE

Vital. Teachers, careers officers, doctors, parents or religious leaders may be able to give expert advice based on years of experience or training.

RIGHT

The right decision is the decision that's right for *you*. And only you can make it. It can be a disaster to allow yourself to be pushed into the wrong decision by others whose advice, or expectations of you, say more about them than about what's right for you. After all, it's your life!

It's also a mistake to push yourself into the wrong decision, for example because of your own crazy expectations of yourself, or because you don't think about the decision at all.

WHAT

What is the decision/problem/goal exactly?
What do you think is important and right/wrong?
What are the facts?
What are the alternatives and consequences?
What expert advice have you got?

CAN'T?

Can't decide? Don't panic! Good decisions may take time. But putting them off for long may make things worse.

NEXT

It's not 'success' or 'failure' that matter, but our attitude to them.

100

STRESS
EXERCISE
EATING
DRUGS

There's really only one secret of survival in today's world, with its pressures and problems, and that's a healthy lifestyle. Looking and feeling fit and having fun are skills, not luck.

STRESS ▶▶▶

Stress can be good for you!

Healthy stress involves all the normal ups and downs of life (you need the downs to have the ups), but you get over the downs a lot quicker.

HEALTHY

Healthy stress can come from:
- exercise
- healthy eating
- relaxation (walking the dog, yoga . . .)

All addresses in Addresses!

101

- choosing challenges (e.g. courses and work) that are right for *you*

It can show itself in:
- feeling good
- energy
- confidence
- enthusiasm
- happiness

- knowing how to cope
- making good decisions
and so on.

- passing exams
- handling criticism
- being relaxed
- being able to fight back against problems
and so on.

UNHEALTHY

Unhealthy stress can come from things like:
- choosing the wrong options
- choosing the wrong career
- trying to live up to other people's expectations
- training, studying or working too hard or too little
- bottling up problems
- being disorganised
- loneliness

- debt
- not knowing how to deal with relationships
- eating food which is full of chemicals, fat, sugar . . .
- not getting enough exercise
- gambling
and so on.

It can show itself in:
- tiredness
- bad temper
- poor results
- feeling inadequate
- feeling everyone's against you
- being aggressive
- being nervous

- eating too much or too little
- smoking, drinking, taking pills . . .
- feeling you've got a rotten personality
- pain
- poor concentration
and so on.

✎ READING

- *Well Being: Helping Yourself to Good Health* (Penguin): about a healthy lifestyle
- *The Diary of a Teenage Health Freak* (Oxford Paperbacks)
- free leaflets from your local Health Authority's Health Education Unit (in Northern Ireland, from your Health and Social Services Board's unit): on the subjects in this chapter

EXERCISE ▶▶▶

Why bother? After school, it's easy not to bother. But healthy exercise can help you to loosen up, feel energetic, do things for longer, become strong, get rid of fat, let off steam — in other words most of the things you need to do to survive life after school.

If it sounds like a real bore, forget difficult exercises, expensive sports (or any sports), fitness programmes, aerobics etc. Healthy exercise is simple and for everyone and for life. A regular mixture of simple activities is all you need:
■ getting off the bus/train a stop early
■ walking, swimming, cycling (three great fitness activities)
■ dancing: disco, ballroom, jazz, tap, ballet, folk, break . . .
and so on.

You don't need expensive sports gear. Borrow or hire anything you need, or make do with jeans and trainers. These days who cares what you wear, as long as it's safe?

Leisure centres and sports clubs have a lot to offer, but you don't have to join them. Friends, workmates, or family may want to exercise too, but you don't have to join them either. It's up to you.

CONTACTS
■ your local library has addresses of all local sports clubs
■ your national Sports Council can put you in touch with people doing any sport you're interested in
■ your doctor: get expert advice about exercise after illness or an operation

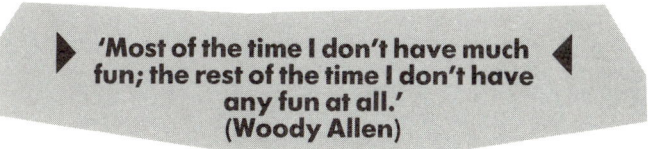

▶ 'Most of the time I don't have much ◀
fun; the rest of the time I don't have
any fun at all.'
(Woody Allen)

EATING ▶▶▶

You become what you eat.

Healthy eating helps to reduce spots, weight, greasy hair, tooth decay, fat, and tiredness, and to avoid heart trouble, bowel trouble and cancer.

Healthy eating in 60 seconds!

More fibre
More fruit and vegetables, baked beans (Beans Meanz Health), wholemeal bread, bran and wholewheat breakfast cereals, peas, sweetcorn, brown rice, boiled potatoes . . .

Less fat
Less butter, full-cream milk, fatty meat, greasy and fried food (including chips), cheese . . .

Less sugar
Less jam, chocolate, tinned food, sugar, cake, sauce, fizzy and boozy drink . . .

Less salt
Less sauce, packet food (including soups and crisps), salt, processed food . . .

OK
Fresh fruit, fresh vegetables, wholemeal bread, skimmed and semi-skimmed milk, boiled potatoes, yoghurt, fish, white meat, clear soups, brown rice, cottage cheese, low-calorie drinks, seafood . . .

Tips
- grilling avoids all the fat of frying
- more fibre makes you feel less hungry
- fresh food has no chemicals such as artificial preservatives, artificial colourings, or artificial flavourings (often marked on packets as E numbers, e.g. E150)
- raw or steamed vegetables keep their vitamins
- try healthier take-aways with a low fat filling: baked potato, wholemeal pizza, wholemeal bread sandwiches . . .
- if you learn how to cook, you can cut down on packet foods and tins
- ask for healthier food at home, school, and work
- compare the amounts of fibre, fat, sugar and salt by checking the 'nutritional information' on the side of the packet; for example:
  Ordinary milk 22g of fat per pint
  Semi-skimmed milk 11g of fat per pint
  Skimmed milk 1g of fat per pint

Forget the boring calorie charts and diets. Healthy eating is simple and for everyone and for life. In a few days or weeks, the unhealthy food that tastes good now may start tasting rotten. A combination of simple foods is all you need to get a good mixture of:

- carbohydrates   - vitamins
- fats   - minerals
- protein

Food provides energy, measured in calories. If the body doesn't need energy it has to store it as fat. If it hasn't got enough energy, it uses up the fat. Getting to, and staying at, a weight that's right for you, is usually only a matter of having a lifestyle with regular exercise, healthy eating and healthy stress. Eating a lot less, or a lot more, to deal with a weight problem is hopeless, because you'll either give it up after a while, or it'll become a dangerous obsession.

CONTACT

- your doctor if you think you are too fat or too thin (also ask about self-help groups; see page 147); and if you have a baby (your own diet isn't safe for your baby)

DRUGS ▶▶▶

'One reason I don't drink is that I want to know when I'm having a good time' said Nancy Astor, Britain's first woman MP.

WHAT

Drugs are things like alcohol, coffee, cigarettes, tranquillisers, medicines, pills, glue and harder drugs that help speed up or slow down the working of your body and mind. Doctors know what they're giving you, so do chemists. Other people may not know or care as long as they get your money, or a laugh out of you.

WHY

There are many reasons why people use drugs:
- pressure from advertisers and friends
- stress, loneliness, lack of confidence, wanting to feel grown up
- the atmosphere of pubs and discos
and so on.

Spotting these hidden influences in your life could stop you starting, or start you stopping, or at least help you to control the situation.

LAW

You know already that the law has to come down like a ton of bricks on people using, keeping, or selling harder drugs like speed, heroin, methadone, LSD, cocaine. *But* just because the law says it's OK to use other drugs in moderation doesn't mean they're safe. That's why it's also illegal to drive after more than a couple of very small glasses of booze, or to bring drink to the match.

RISKS

Many experts are afraid of boring or frightening people (or making them more interested) by droning on about the risks. But to put it simply:
- once you start, even for a laugh, it can easily become a habit you can't do without; you become hooked/addicted, and the problems snowball; you think you're controlling the drug, but it's controlling you
- you risk your health and life: lung cancer, heart disease and bronchitis from smoking; putting air into your blood stream or picking up AIDS (see page 131) by injecting harder drugs; losing your balance, judgment and self-control by drinking; choking on vomit or plastic bags by glue-sniffing . . .
- you risk the health and life of others: your baby's health during and after pregnancy; other people's health from smoking near them; other people's lives by causing an accident or influencing them to start misusing drugs . . .

SAFE

Just common sense. Mixing drugs, smoking cigarettes, using glue or taking harder drugs are just too risky. Pills, tranquillisers and medicines must be used according to the instructions. Two or three small (standard) drinks, two or three times a week, at the right time and in the right place, are probably OK, but need handling like dynamite. Coffee is OK as long as you don't drink too much.

1 standard drink =

| 1 half pint of beer | 1 single whisky | 1 glass of wine | 1 glass of sherry |

CONTACTS

- dial 100 and ask the operator for 'Freefone Drug Problems' (it's free). You can also speak to your local Drug Advice Service
- doctor (see page 145)
- hospital (see page 146)
- see page 147

MONEY

You *can* avoid money problems.

BUDGETING ▶▶▶

As soon as you get a training allowance, giro, pay-packet or grant the easiest thing is to blow the whole lot, and end up broke or in debt. You can avoid that by budgeting. That means looking at your weekly income, spending and saving (!) and working out a *realistic* weekly money plan.

108

All addresses in Addresses!

BUDGET OPTIONS

Income
Training Allowance £28.50

Spending
Parents	£10.00
Lunches	£ 3.35
Train	£ 2.90
Leisure Centre	£ 1.00
Books, newspapers, magazines	£ 2.00
Hair-cut (year divided by 52 weeks)	£ 0.75
Records/tapes (divided by 52)	£ 2.00
Clothes (divided by 52)	£ 1.75
Video tape	£ 2.00
Total	
	£25.75

Saving
£ 2.75

INCOME

More:

- checking that you're claiming all training allowances, benefits and grants that you are entitled to
- changing jobs
- another job as well (e.g. self-employment)
- interest from a savings account

and so on.

SPENDING

Less:

- walking!
- special offers on food in shops and markets, especially on food which goes bad quickly, which may be sold cheaply on its 'sell by' date, or in the late afternoon, or Saturday afternoon

- packed lunches
- shopping around: the same record or pair of jeans may be on sale at a dozen different prices in one streeet
- cheap travel deals (see page 152)
- second-hand clothes, books, blankets, beds, furniture, records, cookers etc. from junk shops, jumble sales, adverts (in newspapers and on college noticeboards), auctions and charity shops
- buying food which carries a supermarket's own name on the label
- buying in bulk: you could also pool your money with others
- buying good quality things: if they cost twice as much but last four times as long, they're cheaper in the long run
- asking for reductions for young or unemployed people or students at leisure centres, hairdressers, cafes . . . (you may have to show your signing-on card or student union card)
- learning to spot the con men before they spot you!

and so on.

SAVING

If you put a few pounds into a savings account each week, you'll have money for travel, a posh suit/dress or a stereo and you'll be able to show a bank or building society that you're careful with money, which will make it a lot easier to borrow money to buy things like a car or flat later on. You'll also earn interest. Don't save too much, though — you're only young once!

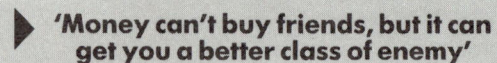

▶ 'Money can't buy friends, but it can get you a better class of enemy' ◀

S E R V I C E S ▶▶▶

WHY

A bank account is needed to turn a training allowance, wage or grant cheque into cash. But there are many other services you can get from banks, building societies, and the Post Office (National Savings Bank and National Giro Bank).

HOW

You can open an account with £1. It doesn't matter what age you are, or if you are unemployed. But first, shop around for the best deal:

- cheaper loans, free services, and special advisors for young people
- calculators, travel cards, discounts on records for new customers (of course free gifts don't make a good bank)
- a bank manager who understands your needs; some are great, some are terrible
- opening times and days that suit you

and so on.

SAVINGS ACCOUNTS

A lot better than money under the bed. The more you save and the longer you leave your savings in your account, the more interest you get. Unlike shares (see page 61), you can't lose money.

Deposit accounts offer a lower rate of interest (e.g. 5% which adds £5 to every £100 you keep in your account for a year) but you can get your money back immediately.

Investment accounts offer a higher rate of interest (e.g. 8%) but it takes a few days or weeks to get your money out.

Interest is normally taxed before you get it. However National Savings (Post Office) Investment Accounts give you all the interest without taxing it. So it's the best deal for people who don't pay tax (e.g. on a low or no income).

CASH CARD

If you're at least 14 you may be able to get a plastic card that lets you withdraw money instantly from a cash machine outside a bank or building society (and at many of its other branches) up to 24 hours a day, seven days a week.

CHEQUE BOOK

A lot safer than a pocket full of bank notes. Ask to open a current account. No interest, but no charge either if there's money in your account. You can write cheques instead of

111

paying cash. And cheques are the only safe way of sending money through the post (apart from Postal Orders which are expensive). However, before you can get much use out of your cheque book, you need a cheque card, a plastic card which guarantees your cheques up to £50. You can't get one until the bank trusts you, which usually means you must be earning money or getting a student grant. Cheques have to be written carefully, and cheque cards should always be kept in a different place from cheque books, otherwise a crook could have an early Christmas at your expense.

INSURANCE

Vital for things like your bike, camera, holiday, rented TV, motorbike and car, in case of loss, theft, damage, and accident. There are special types of insurance for whatever you want to insure. Shop around for the best deal, but read the small print twice to make sure you are properly covered. Student unions, student travel offices, and insurance brokers (see Yellow Pages under Insurance) may offer the best deal of all.

LOANS

It's getting easier to borrow money, but it's still very difficult to pay it back. About half a million people in this country have debt problems. If you haven't enough money, it's better to wait until you have.

If you must borrow, try to get a loan from your parents or relatives (although mixing relationships and money can lead to trouble). Otherwise try to get interest-free credit from a shop, or ask for a bank overdraft. You have to be at least 18, or a parent has to act as a guarantor (to cough up if you can't). Make sure you can afford all the loan repayments, not just the first few. But first ask yourself whether you want to spend so much on one thing. *If you do get into debt, don't borrow any more money*, but get advice from your local Citizens Advice Bureau (address in phone book).

Interest

The real interest rate is called the Annual Percentage Rate, and you must be told the APR by law. The lower it is, the cheaper the loan. An APR of 30% means that you have to pay back an extra

£30 for every £100 you borrow for a year. So a £100 stereo paid back over several years could cost up to £200. 30% APR is high, and anything higher should be avoided like the plague. If in doubt, have a loan agreement checked by a local Citizens Advice Bureau.

Banks

Bank interest rates are usually as low as you will find anywhere, and may not be far above the lowest interest rates allowed by the government. But the bank will want to know how you can pay back the loan, and what (security) they can take from you if you can't. A bank overdraft means you ask for permission to write cheques for more money than you have in your current account. It's often the quickest and cheapest loan of all. A bank personal loan, with a fixed time to pay it back and a fairly low interest rate, is very useful for some larger expenses (e.g. travel or a car). A bank ordinary loan is for a very large amount. It must be paid back within about three years. You can also get a bank mortgage (see below).

Building Societies

You may be able to get a special loan (mortgage) to buy a flat or house. The loan will be up to three times your yearly income, perhaps more if you live with someone else who is earning. Normally they lend to people with a good record of saving regular amounts for at least two years. Ask about the government-backed Homeloan Scheme.

Also

- credit cards such as Access and Barclaycard. If you repay the money within a few weeks you don't have to pay any interest at all
- shop budget cards offered by many high street shops
- hire purchase means paying by instalments. The goods don't belong to you (so you can't sell them) until you've paid all the instalments
- money lenders may charge scandalously high interest rates, and are best avoided

READING

- *Moneyfacts* (Careers and Occupational Information Centre (COIC))
- *Shop Around for Credit* (free leaflet from any Citizens Advice Bureau)
- *How to Cope with Credit and Deal with Debt* (Unwin)

TAX

Money you have to pay to the government to pay for roads, schools, defence . . .

Your employer should take tax off your wages, under the PAYE (Pay As You Earn) system. If you are self-employed, you have to pay your own tax by filling in a Tax Return. Employers need to know your tax code (which depends on your allowances, e.g. mortgage interest or children) in order to deduct the right amount of tax. Your tax code is written on a small form called a P45. If it's your first job, apply for a P45 through your employer; in the meantime you may have to pay extra tax under an emergency tax code. Once your P45 arrives, you pay normal tax, and may get a refund of any extra tax paid under the emergency code. When you leave a job, or stop claiming benefits, ask your employer or claims office for your P45, as your new employer will need it. If your situation changes (e.g. through marrying or having children) tell your employers or tax office.

NATIONAL INSURANCE

Money you have to pay to the government to pay for benefits. Your employer should take it off your wages. If you are self-employed you have to pay it yourself. You should be given a National Insurance Number and Card before you leave school, but if not you can get one from your local Department of Health and Social Security Office. The amount you pay depends on your income. In 1987–88 it went from 0–9% of your income; 0% (or nothing) if you were earning less than a 'lower earnings limit'.

There are four different sorts of National Insurance Contributions:

114

- Class 1 if you're employed
- Class 2 if you're self-employed
- Class 3 if you're worried about not paying enough contributions
- Class 4 if you're self-employed and have profits over a certain amount

TAX

Depends on:

A   Your income for the year
That means all earnings (and some types of benefit received) during the Tax Year (April 6th to the following April 5th).

B   Your tax-free allowances for the year
Everybody is allowed to keep a certain amount of their income without paying tax on it. In 1987/88 the allowances for a single person were £2425, and for a single parent or married person £3795. There are extra allowances for single parents, blind people, elderly people . . .

C   Your tax-free expenses for the year
Interest on mortgages up to £30,000 is allowed against tax. Self-employed people can sometimes have their heating, postage, stationery and travel costs knocked off their tax bill.

D   The % rate of income tax
It was 27% in 1987–88 (you pay the government 27p out of every taxable £1 that you earn),

Your yearly tax = A−(B+C), and then multiply the result by D.

Example
A	if your yearly income is	£4000
B	if your yearly tax-free personal allowances are	£2425
C	if your yearly tax-free expenses are	£0
D	if the % rate of income tax is	27%

£4000−(£2425+£0) = £1575, and then multiply by 27% £425.25. Success!

If you earn less than your allowances and expenses added together (e.g. if you're on the dole) you pay nothing.

 CONTACT

- local tax office (see phone book under Inland Revenue)

 READING

- *Moneyfacts: For Young Workers* (Careers and Occupational Information Service (COIC))
- *Income Tax and School Leavers* (free leaflet from local tax office or careers office)
- *Starting in Business* (free leaflet from local tax office)
- *Students and Income Tax* (National Union of Students (NUS))
- free leaflets on National Insurance from any main Post Office or Department of Health and Social Security Office

C O M P L A I N I N G ▶▶▶

Shoes that last five minutes? Rotten holidays? Stereo that keeps breaking down? Overcharging? Bad food? By law, you don't have to put up with them:

- speak to the manager of the shop (not the manufacturer)
- bring your receipt (but you don't need one by law)
- claim a refund: you don't have to accept a replacement, repair or credit note (guarantees, shop signs, what the manager says, buying in sales or buying second-hand can't change your rights)
- if you're still not happy, contact one of the organisations below
- but remember that you don't have many rights if you buy from private sellers, jumble sales, charity shops, or auctions, or if you simply don't want, don't like, or have damaged something

 CONTACTS

- local Citizens Advice Bureau
- local Consumer Advice Centre
- local Trading Standards Office
- a trade association (such as the Association of British Travel Agents (ABTA) for travel agents)

 READING

- *Consumerfacts* (Careers and Occupational Information Centre (COIC))

116

BENEFITS

WHAT
HOW

You can claim benefits if you haven't got enough money to live on. It's your income that counts, not your parents' income.

For most benefits you have to be at least 16; for some you have to pay National Insurance Contributions first (see page 114); for others you must have very little money; but there are some benefits without conditions attached.

Here is a brief guide to the main benefits at the time of writing. However, you are advised to confirm these details with your local DHSS office, and to ask about any new developments.

WHAT ▶▶▶

INCOME SUPPORT

If you are at least 16 and have little or no money coming in. However, if you are 16 or 17 and refuse youth training, it isn't likely that you'll get it. Students can claim it during the long holidays only. You may be able to get extra weekly payments to pay for a hostel, board and lodgings (but see page 137), and special 'premiums', e.g. if you are disabled or have children. You may also be able to get a loan from your local benefit office's Social Fund for your special expenses such as blankets or a cooker.

UNEMPLOYMENT BENEFIT

If you're unemployed and have paid enough Class 1 National Insurance Contributions. It lasts for one year only, but you can claim Income Support after that.

HOUSING BENEFIT

If you're at least 16 and on a low income or benefits. It's to help pay your rent and rates. If you rent from a private landlord you get a cheque from your local council Housing Benefits Office. If you rent from the local council (in Northern Ireland, the Housing Executive) your rent and rates are reduced. If you live in a hostel or a bed and breakfast hotel you get extra Income Support instead. Students renting from private landlords can claim it too.

HEALTH BENEFITS

If you're claiming Income Support or Family Credit, or are pregnant or have a child under five, you can claim:
- free dental treatment
- free prescriptions at the chemist
- refund of hospital fares
- see page 145

CRISIS LOAN

You may be able to claim it if:
- you're waiting for benefits
- you haven't got your first wages yet
- your benefits have been stopped
- you're homeless, robbed, flooded out, broke . . .

118

Who (examples)

- unemployed and haven't worked long or at all
- paying rent/rates and on low income or benefits
- training, studying or working part-time
- living in a hostel or bed and breakfast and on a low income or benefits
- desperate for money, with no one to help you
- unemployed after working for some time

- on a low income and bringing up children
- sick and off work
- pregnant

- bringing up children
- single parent
- disabled
- need medical treatment and on benefits
- unemployed student during summer holiday
- student in private rented accommodation

Benefits (examples)

Income Support
Housing Benefit
Income Support
Income Support

Crisis Loan
Unemployment Benefit
Family Credit
Sickness Benefit
Maternity Allowance
Child Benefit
One Parent Benefit
Disability Benefits
Health Benefits
Income Support
Housing Benefit

MATERNITY ALLOWANCE

If you are pregnant, can't get Statutory Maternity Pay from an employer (see page 67), but have been employed or self-employed recently, and have been paying Class 1 or Class 2 National Insurance Contributions (see page 114), you can get Maternity Allowance for up to 18 weeks.

MATERNITY PAYMENT (FROM THE SOCIAL FUND)

If you get Income Support or Family Credit, and are pregnant or have a child up to three months old, you can get a special can get a special payment to help with your expenses. If your savings are over £500, the payment may be reduced.

CHILD BENEFIT

If you're a parent. If you're under 16 or under 19 and at school/college, your parents can claim it for you.

ONE PARENT BENEFIT

If you're a single parent.

FAMILY CREDIT

If you work but have a low income, and have children, you can get this extra weekly payment.

SICKNESS BENEFIT

If you can't get Statutory Sick Pay from an employer (see page 67), and if you have paid enough National Insurance Contributions, you can get Sickness Benefit for up to 28 weeks. After that you can get Invalidity Benefit. If you can't get those, you can get Income Support.

DISABILITY BENEFITS

You may be able to claim:
- Attendance Allowance: at any age, if you need someone to look after you
- Mobility Allowance: at any age, if you can't, or almost can't, walk
- Severe Disablement Allowance: if you're at least 16 and can't work

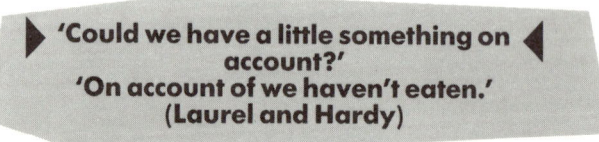

▶ 'Could we have a little something on ◀
account?'
'On account of we haven't eaten.'
(Laurel and Hardy)

HOW ▶▶▶

Claim immediately or you'll lose benefit. If you're not sure whether you are entitled to a benefit, claim it anyway. Remember you can get different types of benefit at the same time, e.g. Unemployment Benefit and Housing Benefit.

UNDER 18

If you want to claim Supplementary or Unemployment Benefit, go to your local careers office and register for work. They give you a card to take to your local Department of Employment/ Unemployment Benefit Office. When you go there, bring your National Insurance Number and P45 (see page 114) if you have them. They give you a form to fill in and post to your local Department of Health and Social Security (DHSS) Office.

AT LEAST 18

If you want to claim Income Support or Unemployment Benefit, go to your local Department of Health and Social Security (DHSS) Office or Department of Employment/Unemployment Benefit Office, and say you want to claim benefit. Bring your National Insurance Number and P45 (see page 114) if you have them.

EVERYONE

If you want to claim any other benefit (except Housing Benefit), visit, phone or write to your local Department of Health and Social Security (DHSS) Office (writing may be best).

For Housing Benefit, claim at your local council Housing Benefit Office (in Northern Ireland, your local Housing Executive Office). But if you're claiming Income Support or Unemployment Benefit, ask your Benefit Office how to claim Housing Benefit.

For Income Support or Unemployment Benefit, keep signing on every fortnight on the day and at the time written on your signing-on card. They will send you a cheque by post as soon as you sign. If you can't sign on (e.g. disabled or looking after children) you get a special book or orders to cash at a Post Office.

CAREFUL!

If you leave a job without good reason, or turn down all Youth Training/job offers, your Income Support or Unemployment Benefit could be stopped or cut for several weeks.

DESPERATE

If you're desperate for money, visit or phone your local Social Security Office and explain your needs (at weekends also try phoning the local council Social Services Department).

DELAY

Delays can happen. Don't let them forget you.

HASSLE

Benefit staff are under pressure. Why not pick a quiet time of the day to telephone or visit the Benefit Office. Speak to the supervisor if you're not getting anywhere.

WORKING

You can still get Income Support or Unemployment Benefit, but tell your claims office as soon as you start work (e.g. voluntary work or part-time work). You'll be allowed to earn at least £5 a week (maybe a lot more) plus enough to cover your travel and other expenses (special clothes and tools, and very cheap meals).

TRAINING OR STUDYING

If it's for less than 12 hours, you can still get Income Support. After three months (if you change your course slightly), or when you're 19, or have finished Youth Training, you can train/study up to 21 teaching hours, and do as much private studying as you like.

HOLIDAY/JOB-FINDING

You can go away for a few weeks, but you must fill in a Holiday Form *before* you leave.

REFUSED?

- have you claimed the right benefit?
- have you given them all the facts they need?
- do *they* understand the rules?
- if they still won't pay, you can appeal to a Social Security Appeal Tribunal, or Housing Benefit Appeal Board, by writing an appeal letter. (Say you wish to appeal. Ask them to send to you two copies of the appeal papers, one for you and one for your representative. Tell them your National Insurance number.) If you go to the Tribunal, you can bring along a friend, relative or someone from your local Citizens Advice Bureau for support. It's informal and held in private, so don't worry.

CONTACTS

- dial 100 and ask the operator for 'Freefone DHSS' (it's free); ask any question
- local Citizens Advice Bureau
- local Law Centre
- local council Welfare Rights Office (at the Social Services Department)

READING

Free leaflet on Housing Benefit from your local council Housing Benefit Office, and free leaflets from your local Social Security Office, or the DHSS Leaflets Unit, such as:

- *Young People's Guide to Social Security*
- *Which Benefit*
- *Babies and Benefits*
- *You Can Appeal*
- *Part-time Work*
- *Sick or Disabled*
- *Voluntary Work*

RELATIONSHIPS

YOU
SUCCESS
SEX

Relationships can be fun, loving, or treacherous. But they matter.

YOU ▶▶▶

Adverts, videos, pop stars and magazines can encourage you to believe that to be 'normal' you have to be slim, beautiful, tall, tough, clever, cool, fun, smart, rich, successful . . . That can also encourage you to spend a fortune on make-up and clothes, lie about relationships, sleep around, risk your life on dangerous stunts, smoke or stop eating, all in a hopeless attempt to live up to these images.

The truth is that real people have problems: spots, fat, failures, bad moods, worries, times of loneliness. *These* things are normal. You are normal.

124

All addresses in Addresses!

The skill of making a success of relationships has never been more important. One out of every three marriages ends in divorce, with pain for all involved, including the children.

FRIENDS

As the saying goes: 'to have a friend you have to be a friend', helping, sharing, caring, and being loyal, through the good times and the bad. And even if you have a close relationship, it makes sense not to lose touch with friends, in case your relationship ends.

PARENTS/GUARDIANS/RELATIVES

Most people go through bad patches at home. The difference between love and interference is not always easy to see. But getting along with parents is a skill that can be learnt.

But if there's serious trouble of *any* sort, especially if you're being attacked or sexually abused, don't put up with it. Threaten to report what's happening. Phone an advice service like Childline. And, if necessary, get help. There is absolutely no shame in getting help. See page 147.

If parents separate or divorce, and there's a disagreement about which parent should look after the children, the court has to decide on 'custody'. The children can tell the court which parent they would rather live with, but the court also has to decide what is in the children's best interest. The court can also decide how often the other parent can have 'access' to (see) the children.

MEN AND WOMEN

A successful relationship should be based on caring and sharing.

Marriage is a very big emotional and legal step, and simply wanting it as a way to leave home, or feel grown up, isn't likely to be enough for success. Many say that marriage is the only solid rock on which to build a relationship, helping people to get through the bad times, and providing a secure home for children. Many others argue that it can take ages before anyone knows what a person is *really* like, and that it's better to live with someone first.

125

MEN AND MEN; WOMEN AND WOMEN

Some people say that a sexual relationship between people of the same sex (homosexuality) is 'wrong'. Others say that it's as 'right' and as loving and caring as any other. Why not discuss your feelings with someone who won't try to force their opinions on you (see page 147)? You can also contact a group giving information, advice and help to gays (men) and lesbians (women) (see page 147).

BREAK UP

A clear, quick and honest break up is better than a messy, drawn out and deceitful break up. Unfortunately once a relationship ends one or both sides can jump to crazy conclusions, feeling that they've been 'rejected'. Time helps to heal wounds, and the lessons learnt can lead to a better relationship.

ALONE

Many people prefer to be alone a lot of the time. That is normal. Of course it's great to have friends too. You can meet people through training workshops, college, work, youth clubs, unemployment centres, leisure centres, sports clubs, pressure groups, political parties, voluntary groups, youth hostels . . .

SECRETS

- not confusing love with sex
- not confusing the real person with their looks or success
- trusting, and being trustworthy
- partners respecting each other
- not playing hurtful games
- partners accepting each other for what they are, not what they would like each other to be
- each partner recognising his/her own faults
- talking about problems, not bottling them up
- partners knowing what they both mean by 'right' and 'wrong' (see page 97)

- working at a relationship through the bad times; it's a bad relationship that doesn't survive the bad times; but a relationship that does survive the bad times can be better than before
- partners recognising and understanding each other's needs, feelings and moods: for example, women can become tense, moody and easily upset before or during their monthly periods (Pre-Menstrual Tension (PMT) and period pains)
- learning about sex and pregnancy

and so on.

CONTACTS

- parents, friendly teachers, trustworthy friends, youth workers, religious leaders . . .
- Childline: about any problem
- a social worker at your local council Social Services Department (in Scotland, Social Work Department): about any serious problem with parents (under 17 you could be taken into care)
- National Society for the Prevention of Cruelty to Children (NSPCC): about any serious problem with parents
- your local Marriage Guidance Council (you don't have to be married): about any family problem (not just marriage)
- local Gay Switchboard (see phone book): also the Gay Switchboard in London
- Lesbian and Gay Youth Movement
- see page 147.

READING

- *Parents and Teenagers* (Unwin)
- *When Parents Split Up* (Chambers)
- *Cohabitation Handbook* (Pluto Press): about living together without marriage
- *So You Think You Are Attracted To The Same Sex?* (Penguin)

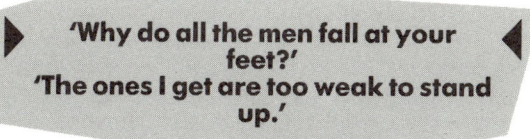

'Why do all the men fall at your feet?'
'The ones I get are too weak to stand up.'

There's a lot more to relationships than sex. But sex is an important part of many relationships.

RUBBISH!

There's a lot of rubbish talked about sex:
■ it isn't true that men are more interested in sex than women
■ it isn't true that everyone is having sex
■ it isn't true that a woman won't become pregnant the first time she has sex

READY?

Getting the best from a relationship involving sex means being ready for the relationship and the sex:
■ not being under pressure from yourself (false ideas), or from your partner
■ not being under the control of drugs
■ understanding your partner's feelings and emotions
■ having a sense of responsibility for your own actions

LAW

■ sex must be by clear agreement, otherwise it's a very serious crime (rape) causing very serious emotional and often physical damage
■ it is illegal for a man to have sex with a girl under 16 (17 in Northern Ireland)
■ sex between men under 21 is illegal
■ sex with a brother, sister, father, mother, uncle, aunt, grandfather or grandmother is a serious crime (incest)

CONTRACEPTION/BIRTH CONTROL

Six out of every 10 teenage women are pregnant when they marry. Many thousands of pregnant teenage mothers and fathers-to-be wish they'd used contraception. Some people say it's wrong. Many people say it's an essential part of modern life.

Obviously you can kiss, cuddle, touch and fondle (heavy petting), without having sex. But if a man's sperms come anywhere near a woman's vagina, they can cause pregnancy. So if you don't want to become pregnant, you must use contraception.

Contraception is the responsibility of the woman *and the man*.

There are only a few very safe/reliable methods. They are shown below and listed on page 130. Most other so called 'methods' are not reliable. You can get a condom (also called a sheath, rubber, johnny or French letter) from chemists and many other shops. You can get all contraceptives (free) from your local Family Planning Clinic, but they *may* want the agreement of your parents if you are under 16.

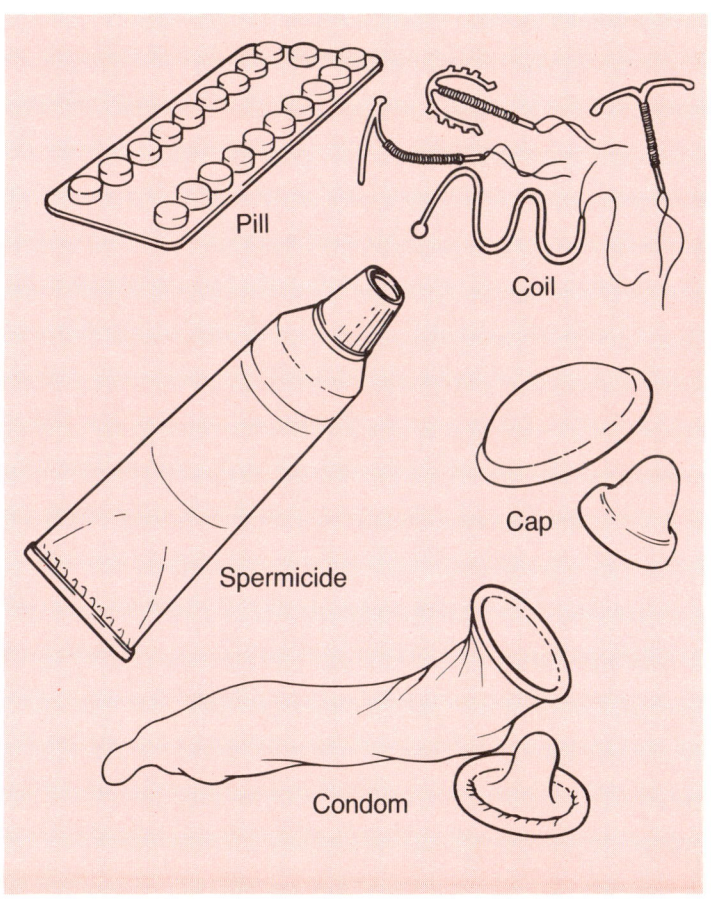

Pill

Coil

Cap

Spermicide

Condom

MAIN METHODS OF CONTRACEPTION/BIRTH CONTROL

Condom
Used by men. A thin rubber sheath (also called a rubber/johnny/French letter) which the man rolls onto his erect penis before sex to prevent the sperm entering the vagina. From local Family Planning Clinics (free), and now widely available in chemists and other shops (inexpensive). A successful method when used properly.

Pill
Used by women. A pill taken to stop the woman producing eggs. From a doctor, who will say which one is most suitable and explain how to take it. It's a very successful method if taken correctly.

Cap
Used by women. A soft rubber cap (also called a diaphragm) which the woman puts inside her vagina before sex to stop sperm entering her womb. From a doctor or local Family Planning Clinic. Quite a successful method, but more successful when used with spermicide (from a chemist or local Family Planning Clinic).

Coil
Used by women. A small coil (also called an Inter-Uterine Device/IUD) put inside the woman's womb by a doctor to stop the fertilised egg from settling in the womb. A very successful method, but it can cause pain at first, and it is not usually suitable for young women.

Spermicide
A cream (available from a chemist or Family Planning Clinic) which destroys sperms. Not successful enough to be used on its own, but it does provide additional protection when used with the sheath or cap.

PREGNANT

If a woman misses her periods, has sore breasts, feels sick or dizzy, or puts on weight, it *may* mean she's pregnant. A doctor or local Family Planning Clinic or the nearest Brook Advisory Centre can do a simple pregnancy test.

A child brings great rewards, but also great responsibilities: responsibilities not to smoke, drink, catch sexual diseases, or do anything else that could damage the child before and after birth, and also to give the child all the love, care, and time that children need.

130

Happy?

If a woman is happy to be pregnant she needs all the expert information, advice and help from a doctor to protect her and her baby. There are special clinics/classes for pregnant mothers and fathers-to-be. A pregnant woman also has rights at work (see page 67) and rights to benefits (see page 119).

Unhappy?

If a woman is not happy to be pregnant, she needs expert information, advice and help immediately. Her options are to:
- keep her baby: the father, her parents, relatives and friends may be much more helpful than expected
- give her baby to someone else for adoption
- stop the pregnancy in a hospital (abortion): many people think it's wrong; many people think a woman should have the right to choose; it has to be done as soon as possible, so it's important to see a doctor immediately; if the woman is under 16 her parents must agree to the abortion.

DANGERS

Sexually Transmitted Diseases

AIDS is a killer disease that can't be cured at the time of writing. It stops the body's defences from fighting diseases. Its full name is Acquired Immunity Deficiency Syndrome. It isn't only transmitted sexually. It can be transferred, through body fluids such as semen and blood, from one person to another. It has spread particularly amongst homosexual men, but it can be passed from any infected man or woman to any other man or woman. Drug abusers are also at risk if they share needles.

VDs or venereal diseases such as gonorrhoea or syphilis, are spread by sex with infected men and women. Each year gonorrhoea is picked up by over 25,000 people under 24. Many VDs don't show symptoms for some time. Most can be cured, and the sooner they are treated, the better the chances of limiting any damage.

You can cut the risk of catching AIDS or VD by:
- using a condom/sheath/rubber/johnny/French letter
- having sex with one person only, or as few people as possible
- not sharing drug needles

131

- dicussing AIDS and VD with your partner; if there is any reason to suspect that one of you might be infected, you have a responsibility not to have sex, and to go for a check up immediately (see below).

Signs of infection include: itching, sores and rashes near sex organs, pain when passing water, unusual discharge, diarrhoea, sweating and skin problems. Obviously these don't prove that you have a disease, but if you have any doubts, go immediately for a check up at a Sexually Transmitted Disease (STD) Clinic. Many people use these clinics, so you won't be alone or embarrassed.

Cervical Cancer

All women having sex should have a (smear) test from a doctor or local Family Planning Clinic every three years. It's a simple and quick test for early signs of cancer at the neck of the womb (cervix). The cancer can be cured if spotted early.

CONTACTS

- doctor (see page 145)
- local Family Planning Clinic (see phone book under F)
- nearest Brook Advisory Centre for young people (see phone book under B): birth control/contraception advice, pregnancy testing, help with sexual and emotional problems
- British Pregnancy Advisory Service (see phone book under B)
- Ulster Pregnancy Advisory Association (see phone book under U)
- local council Social Services Department: for emergency housing if you're pregnant, and for adoption
- nearest Sexually Transmitted Disease (STD) Clinic (also called Genito-Urinary (GU) Clinics, Special Clinics and Special Treatment Centres) (see phone book under Venereal Disease or Sexually Transmitted Disease, or under the name of your nearest large hospital)
- local Rape Crisis Centre (see phone book under R): also the Rape Crisis Centre in London
- New Grapevine: about incest

READING

- leaflets and books about birth control: from your local Family Planning Clinic, Family Planning Association or Family Planning Information Service

132

- *Safe Sex for Teenagers* (Brook Advisory Centres)
- *Talking Sex* (Piccolo)
- *Make it Happy: What Sex is all About* (Penguin)
- *The Pregnancy Book* (Health Education Council): free from your local health authority's Health Education Unit
- *Single and Pregnant* (National Council for One-Parent Families)

HOME

STAYING
LEAVING
FINDING
HOMELESS
SUCCESS

Right now, thousands of people are discovering that home was far more important than they thought: they're young, broke, lonely, dirty, and ill, sleeping rough in unfriendly cities.

But you CAN make a success of leaving home, by proper planning.

STAYING ▶▶▶

WHY

- cheaper
- very difficult to find somewhere (even a hostel)
- rented rooms can be cramped and lonely
- can't claim benefits without an address

All addresses in addresses!

- easier to find a new home from an old one
- if you leave, you'll have to pay all the bills, do all the washing, and put up with new rules from landlords (about parties, noise, visitors, posters, furniture . . .)

and so on.

SECRETS

- not letting others walk all over you
- helping to pay the bills
- helping with the chores
- treating others the way you want to be treated: not too long in the bathroom; keeping the music down; allowing other people their privacy etc.
- getting *yourself* sorted out (work, courses, money, relationships, health . . .) so that you're easier to live with
- getting help if you're living in overcrowded, damp, dirty or dangerous conditions

CONTACTS

- local council Housing Department
- local Citizens Advice Bureau
- National Association for Young People in Care
- Black and In Care

WHY

- freedom
- hassle at home
- trouble at home
- no work near home
- no suitable course near home

and so on.

LAW

- at 16 you can leave home if your parents or a court agree
- at 18 (16 in Scotland) you can leave without permission
- under 17 you could be taken into care by the local council Social Services Department (but that's less likely if you have a job and aren't in 'moral' or 'physical' danger)

135

SECRETS

- staying at home or with friends or relatives until you find somewhere
- arranging a job, or job interviews before you leave home; no job, or a badly paid job, may mean no home, and no home may mean that you're tired and dirty, and not likely to get a job
- saving several hundred pounds: the costs, especially in the south-east of England, and cities (London is a nightmare), can be horrific, with rents *starting* at £25–£50 per person per week for one small room. You'll need at least one month's rent in advance, and a month's rent as a deposit
- asking a parent or relative to act as a guarantor to the landlord (agreeing to pay the rent if you can't)
- claiming benefits to help pay for the deposit and rent in advance, and for the weekly rent and rates
- sharing to save rent, food, and heating costs, and as a good halfway step between leaving home and having your own place
- taking identification, and letting someone know that you're safe, so that they can tell your parents/guardians (e.g. the Message Home Service)

FINDING ▶▶▶

May mean the least disgusting place. Even that is a fight. Many places are snapped up within minutes of an advert appearing. Get a free or cheap street map from an estate agent or tourist office.

WORK

A room, bed-sit or flat that comes free or cheaply with work (armed forces, au pair work, hotel work, child-minding . . .). But if you lose your job, you could lose your home.

PRIVATE LANDLORD

Bed-sits, flats or houses. Some are good, some are unfit for human beings.

LOCAL COUNCIL

Bed-sits, flats or houses. Cheap and often quite good. May be difficult to get, especially if you're under 18. May have a waiting list of up to two years. May be easier to get if you have a special needs (e.g. no parents, kicked out by parents, just out of a hostel, pregnant, have children, a single parent, disabled, ill, or in danger).

HOUSING ASSOCIATION

Bed-sits, flats or houses. May be cheaper than private landlords, but more expensive than local councils. May be easier to get if you have a special needs.

PRIVATE HOME

A room. As a lodger. A good way to start out on your own (e.g. meals and company) if you get a good family.

'HOTEL'

The Hilton? Not unless you see a notice reading 'DHSS welcome'! These 'bed and breakfast hotels' are for the homeless, and classed as 'board and lodgings'. You may get your own room, or have to sleep in a room full of beds. Some are OK, many are terrible. Breakfast may mean nothing more than a packet of cornflakes and tin of powdered milk left outside your door once a week.

HOSTEL

A large room full of beds. Some (youth hostels, YMCA, YWCA) are good, others are terrible. Some help people who have drink or other drug problems, or who need somewhere to stay after prison.

HOUSING CO-OP

Rooms, bed-sits, flats and houses. A group of people who take over a house or street and rent out to their own members.

SHORT-LIFE HOUSING

Flats and houses. Buildings to be demolished or improved, but which are fixed up for a while by housing organisations.

SQUAT

Living in an empty flat, house or other building, without the owner's permission. Get expert advice first. It isn't illegal (except in Scotland) if you do it properly e.g. not doing any damage, and not using electricity/gas without paying for it. Might be worth offering the owner some rent, and trying to become a proper tenant with rights.

COLLEGE

A cheap study-bedroom in a student residence (often with meals), or a bed-sit, flat or house found for you by the college accommodation officer. Apply immediately you get your college place.

BUYING

Buying costs thousands of pounds, e.g. £20,000–£100,000 or more for a small semi-detached house, depending on where it is in the UK. But you may be able to get a special loan to help you to buy (see page 113). Buying works out cheaper than renting, because the place will be yours to keep or sell.

 'It's hard to soar like an eagle when you're living with turkeys.'

CONTACTS

■ friends, relatives, workmates: ask them to keep their eyes and ears open
■ estate agents (see Yellow Pages under Estate Agents)
■ accommodation agency (see Yellow Pages under Accommodation): they may charge anything from £25–£200 for finding you somewhere; they are breaking the law if they charge you a fee before you sign a rental agreement with a landlord
■ local radio accommodaton services

138

- local council Housing Department (in Northern Ireland, your local Housing Executive Office)
- a housing association
- a housing co-operative
- Shelter (an organisation for homeless people)
- Advisory Service for Squatters

W_a READING

- newspapers, as soon as they come out ('Accommodation to Let' and 'Flat-Shares' columns)
- ads in shop windows and on noticeboards at college or work
- *The Lady* magazine: jobs (such as au pair work) with accommodation provided
- *Squatter's Handbook* (Advisory Service for Squatters)

HOMELESS ▶▶▶

Take action early in the day, because any spare beds may be taken quickly, and you could be left to sleep rough

W_a CONTACTS

- youth hostel (see page 159)
- YMCA hostel for men (see the phone book for addresses)
- YWCA hostel for women (see the phone book for addresses)
- local council Housing Department: ask for an interview with a housing officer; explain your needs, especially if you have special needs (see page 137); even if they can't help they must give you information and advice
- hostel or night shelter (address in Yellow Pages under Hostels, or from the local council Housing Department)
- Women's Refuge: for women left homeless after violence at home (address from a Citizens Advice Bureau, local council Social Services Department, or police station)
- London: Piccadilly Advice Centre
- Empty Property Unit: information about short life housing
- Citizens Advice Bureau
- local council Social Services Department (in Scotland, Social Work Department); if you're under 17 you may be taken into care, but if you're 16, they may be able to arrange a local council room or bed-sit, if you're lucky

139

SUCCESS ▶▶▶

It's not over yet!

SECRETS

- checking that you can really afford it. What about hidden costs like heating and rates?
- checking if it's damp or dangerous
- apart from a deposit and advanced rent, don't pay extra money to the landlord (e.g. key money, which is illegal)
- signing a rental agreement (Tenancy Agreement) with the landlord, and having it checked by an expert (see Contacts below). You have fewer rights if it says that the person you rent from is a tenant (sub-letting to you); that the landlord lives in the property or that the agreement is for a short time only
- signing a list ('inventory') with the landlord, of everything in the rooms and checking that everything on the list is really in the rooms and in good condition. If not, and you don't check, you'll have to pay for them when you leave
- getting receipts for the deposit and advanced rent and a rent book (from a newsagent) for the landlord to sign every time you pay your rent. You'll need weekly rent receipts or a rent book to claim Housing Benefit
- checking with the local electricity/gas office whether the landlord is charging too much for electricity/gas
- getting insurance for your belongings (see page 112)
- claiming benefits to help pay your rent and rates (see page 118)
- dealing with landlord trouble immediately, by getting expert help. You (as the tenant) and the landlord have rights and responsibilities. You must stand up for your rights (repairs, fair rent, not to be thrown out unless the landlord has a court order) just as the landlord will stand up for his/her rights (no disturbance, payment of rent, respect for rules etc.)
- knowing where to find and how to use fire extinguishers and fire exits; trying to get flame-proof sofas and beds (foam gives off deadly fumes in a fire); keeping potentially dangerous items such as pills, bleach, boiling kettles, matches, weedkiller away from children; never leaving children alone; never walking alone down badly lit paths; never buying

electrical equipment unless it carries a British Safety mark
(see the logo below) . . .
■ avoiding the trap of cutting yourself off from the outside
world (see page 148)

CONTACTS

■ local Citizens Advice Bureau
■ local Law Centre

■ local council Housing
Department or Housing
Advice Centre

READING

■ leaflets about tenants' rights (free from any Citizens Advice
Bureau or local council Housing Department or Housing
Advice Centre)
■ *Housing Rights Handbook* (Penguin)

You CAN get help with any problem, or help someone else.

EMERGENCY ▶▶▶

ACCIDENT

You could save a life, stop serious injury and help recovery by:
- making sure no one else gets hurt, including you
- not moving the person unless you have to get them out of danger or let them breathe (otherwise you could injure their spine, and that's really serious)
- acting immediately if the person is unconscious (see Save a Life)
- stopping serious bleeding by pressing firmly over the wound, and trying to get a wounded limb above the level of the person's chest

142

All addresses in Addresses!

- loosening tight clothing and making the person comfortable; don't cover them with too many coats or blankets; give nothing to eat or drink
- getting help and then coming back to the person, checking breathing, pulse, and bleeding, and talking calmly and quietly, saying that everything will be OK

SAVE A LIFE

Lay person on his/her back.

A for Airway
Mouth blocked? Look. If mouth blocked:
- scoop out vomit, chewing gum, food etc.
- tilt person's head back, and chin up, to get tongue out of airway

B for Breathing
Breathing? Feel, watch, listen. If not breathing, *but only if not*:
- tilt person's head back
- hold person's nostrils closed
- take deep breath
- make mouth to mouth seal
- blow into person's mouth to raise chest
- remove your mouth
- repeat when person's chest empties (until breathing starts)

C for Circulation
Pulse? Feel wrist, front of neck, veins . . . If no pulse, *but only if none*:
- press down with both hands on centre of person's chest
- pump chest 15 times
- give two breaths (as above)
- repeat (until pulse starts)

R for Recovery
Breathing and pulse? Check. If OK:
- gently turn person on side (this keeps tongue and vomit out of airway)

See A, B, C and R illustrations on page 144.

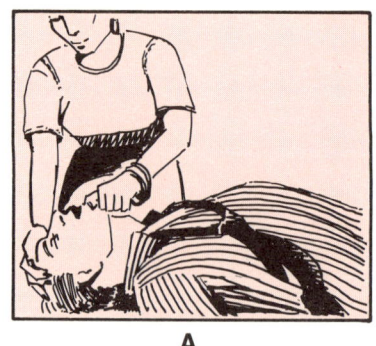

A

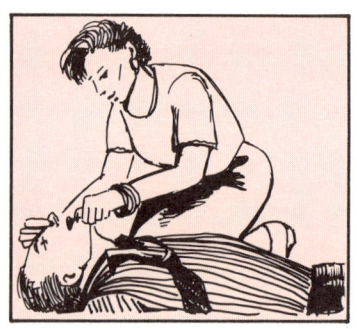

B

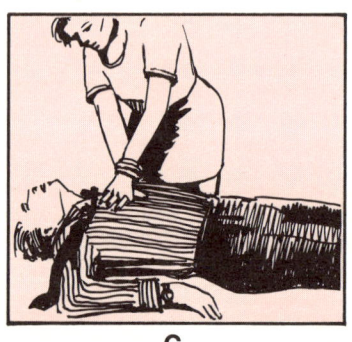

C

R

HELP

Phone 999 (it's free) and ask for Fire, Police, Ambulance or Coastguard:

- say what has happened, what help is needed, and where the emergency services should come
- give your name and address
- give any other information they ask for before leaving the phone

 CONTACT

- British Red Cross: details of your nearest First Aid class

 READING

- *Save a Life* (BBC)
- *First Aid Manual* (Dorling Kindersley)

> ▶ **'Beam me up Scotty!'** ◀

HEALTH ▶▶▶

For free or cheap treatment:

- apply now, through a doctor, for a Health Service Medical Card
- always check that you are being treated under the National Health Service
- say if you are claiming benefits, or on a low income, or pregnant, or have a baby
- give your age: you can get free prescriptions if you are under 16; free dental treatment if you are under 18, or under 19 and in full-time education; vouchers to help pay for glasses if you are under 16, or under 19 and in full-time education

DOCTOR

For all sorts of problems from sleeplessness to serious illness. Register with a doctor (list at your local library) before you are ill. Choose carefully: most are sympathetic to any problem, a few aren't. A recommendation may be the best way to choose. If you need to see the doctor, try to go to the surgery, but if you can't, the doctor will visit you at home. Help the doctor to help you, by mentioning every detail of your problem. It might help to write it all down before you go. Ask the doctor to explain everything clearly, until you understand. Bring a friend if that would help.

HOSPITAL

For minor accidents you can go to a hospital casualty department (open day and night). Not all hospitals have a casualty department – check in your local phone book.

DENTIST

If you're not going to a dentist already, you can choose a dentist from a list at any main Post Office. Have a check-up every six months.

OPTICIAN

If you suffer from regular headaches or blurred vision go for an eye test; they're free.

READING
■ *Patients' Rights* (HMSO)

ANYTHING ▶▶▶

'I've had a great life, I just wish I'd realised it sooner,' said the French writer, Colette. Mark Twain said that he'd known a great many troubles 'but most of them never happened'.

What seems like a big problem, can turn out to be a small problem, especially if you can get help.

SECRETS

■ remembering that many people have problems, worries and moods, even if they don't admit them. You're not alone
■ remembering that you never used to worry about height, spots, hair or weight and in a few years, may never worry again!

146

- asking yourself whether the real problem is crazy expectations of yourself and other people's crazy expectations of you
- remembering that you are 'normal' (whatever that means)
- remembering that there's a lot that's good in your life, and a lot that's good about you
- giving yourself time
- remembering that many people say 'success' is in life's journey, not just one exam result, job interview or relationship

CONTACTS

Many of the experts listed below can help with *any* problem. No matter how trivial, difficult or shocking it seems to you, they'll have heard it before. You don't even have to visit them if you don't want to; just write or phone:
- parents, relatives, friends
- friendly teachers
- youth workers (e.g. at a local youth club or unemployment centre)
- local youth advice (counselling) service (see phone book)
- Childline (see page 125)
- Samaritans (see phone book under Samaritans): every year more than 250,000 people contact the Samaritans for the first time
- a social worker at your local council Social Services Department
- religious leaders (you don't have to be going to their services)
- local Citizens Advice Bureau
- a self-help group: people sharing your problem and getting together to help each other, in groups such as: Alcoholics Anonymous, Gamblers Anonymous, Anorexic Aid (for people with severe problems of undereating), Parents Anonymous (for parents unable to cope) . . . (addresses from your local library)

READING

- phone book: the first few pages are full of useful contacts
- *Sunday Times Self-Help Directory* (Granada)

147

WHAT'S ON

Concerts, films, plays, fashion, video, music . . . why miss out?

If there's nothing happening round your area, make it happen! You shouldn't have to put up with rotten facilities, and end up sitting at home, hanging round the park, or losing your money in arcades (a sure way to get nothing for something).

ORGANISED ▶▶▶

YOUTH GROUPS

You can go along by yourself or with friends. Some are open during the day which is good news if you're unemployed. Facilities and activities include: snooker, cheap snacks, trips to the leisure centre and cheap holidays. Some groups (e.g. at YMCAs) offer opportunities to pick up some skills for life and work. There are also Young Farmers Clubs, open to anyone.

All addresses in Addresses!

MUSIC

There's no need to miss out just because you can't afford LPs or tickets for big concerts. Did you know that you can borrow records and tapes from many local libraries? Did you know that there are up and coming rock, jazz and classical groups playing locally? Why not set up your own band? You could ask for a practice room at a local community centre or youth club, play local venues and send demo-tapes to radio and TV stations.

FILM AND VIDEO

Not just videos or the local cinema. There may be youth club or college film nights and clubs. Why not hire film or video equipment and make your own films? Video is good for documentary work, film is good for creative work; whatever you use, the experts say keep it simple, and rehearse.

TRAVEL

See page 153.

SHOWS, THEATRE, DANCE AND MIME

Not just the local theatre or local disco. You can write to radio/TV station ticket units for free tickets to their shows. There may be local acting (dramatic), dance, and mime groups to watch or join. Local amateur dramatic groups and national youth theatres (e.g. National Youth Theatre and Scottish Youth Theatre) offer you opportunities to act (a great confidence booster), direct, design sets, learn stage lighting.

SPORTS

Even if you hate the idea of sport, there's bound to be something you would like: swimming, snooker, cycling, roller skating, rambling, archery, darts, sailing, self-defence, soccer, dry-slope skiing, fun runs, white water rafting, sport-fighting, cricket, jiu-jitsu, bowls, surfing, judo, ice skating, pool, table tennis. Check out local leisure centres and sports clubs.

VOLUNTEERING

See page 78.

SOCIETIES

School, college, and local societies for photography, painting, astronomy, stamp collecting, gardening, nature, pigeons, cats, motorbikes . . .

MUSEUMS/GALLERIES

May seem boring on a school trip, but if you go alone, and because you want to, it's a different place altogether.

WRITING

You could write about music, conservation, fashion, youth issues, last night's TV or local gigs, for school, youth club, or college magazines, or local newspapers, magazines and radio/TV stations. You could end up with your own column or programme.

LEARNING

Sports, French, photography, dress design, motorcycle maintenance . . . See page 9.

DUKE OF EDINBURGH AWARDS

You can get a bronze, silver or gold award for learning or using a skill: stamp collecting, motorcycle maintenance, life saving, sport, service to the community, adventure expeditions. You can work on your own or in a school group, or youth club. Great for challenge and to boost confidence.

ACTION

See page 172.

SELF-EMPLOYMENT

See page 70.

150

CONTACTS

- local library: details of what's on locally, from clubs to courses, and all useful national and UK addresses
- local council youth officer: details of local youth clubs and events
- your national Sports Council: can put you in touch with people involved in any sport
- local tourist offices: details of many local activities
- local film and video workshops (see Yellow Pages)
- local churches

READING

- local What's On posters
- *The Complete Activity Guide* (Piaktus)
- *Know the Game* books (EP Publishing): archery, billiards, camping, volleyball, yoga etc.
- *Youth Arts and Crafts Book* (I.T. Resources Centre)
- *The Complete Video Handbook* (Penguin)
- *All-In-One Cine Book* (Focal Press)
- *Making Music: Guide to Writing, Performing and Recording* (Pan)
- *Breaks for Young Bands* (Omnibus Press)

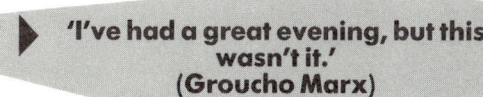

**'I've had a great evening, but this wasn't it.'
(Groucho Marx)**

ORGANISING ▶▶▶

If you're fed up with the local scene, there may be hundreds like you. Why not advertise for people to join you, and get things moving?

IDEAS

- starting a competition: darts, bands, snooker, painting, 5 a side soccer, hockey, chess, gardening . . .
- starting a youth/sports/fan club
- starting a magazine or newspaper about fashion, computing, music . . .
- starting a What's On information service: if you don't know what's on locally, other people won't know either

151

- starting a community activity to bring local people together
- starting a self-help group (see page 147)

PUBLICITY

Hang-gliding down the high street with a loud-hailer, wearing a kilt and a bowler hat? Well maybe not. But anything will do as long as the information is clear, grabs people's attention, and includes all the important times, dates, meeting places and addresses. Examples:

- large coloured posters: ask for permission to put them up in shops, youth clubs, schools, colleges, local libraries, cafes, clinics
- information sheets sent to newspapers or local radio/TV youth and community programmes
- leaflets printed cheaply by local printers or shops
- video or ordinary films
- adverts in local newspapers and shop windows
- exhibitions of your work in schools, youth clubs, libraries, community centres

and so on.

MONEY

You may have to try several things:
- jumble sales
- sponsored walks, runs, parascending, non-stop piano playing
- market stall selling old books, records, clothes
- applying for grants

and so on.

CONTACTS

- local Community Centre: may have a room you could use
- local council: may have a hall to rent
- local businesses: money
- Royal Jubilee Trusts: money
- the Prince's Trust: money
- National Youth Bureau
- your national Youth Clubs Association
- local youth workers

READING

- *Organising Things* (Pluto Press)
- *Community Start-Up* (National Extension College)
- *Organise* (National Association of Youth Clubs)
- *Directory of Grant-Making Trusts* (Charities Aid Foundation)
- *Finding Funds* (National Out of School Alliance)

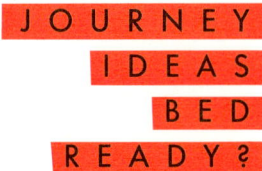

You CAN travel, whether or not you're broke, disabled, training, working, studying ...

If you dream of lying on a tropical beach, under a blazing sun, sipping exotic cocktails and listening to the Walkman, but usually end up on a broken British deck chair in the rain, read on.

JOURNEY ▶▶▶

CHEAPEST

Compare prices first:
- walking!
- cycling (bikes are carried free/cheaply on many trains/ferries)

All addresses in Addresses!

- sharing a car: look for ads on noticeboards at work or college
- cheap day, weekend, weekly or monthly return fares
- under 16, youth, group, unemployed, disabled and student fares (often a half or a third off)
- weekly, monthly, quarterly and yearly season tickets
- rover/explorer tickets for a day, week or month
- cheaper fares during less busy (off-peak) hours, days, (usually Mondays–Thursdays), and (off-season) months (October–April).

and so on.

EVERYONE

If you're studying full-time, it's well worth buying an International Student Identity Card (ISIC). It costs a few pounds and gives you discounts on flights and hotels, and at cinemas and museums. If you're not at school/college, you can buy a Federation of International Youth Travel Organisations (FIYTO) Card for the same sort of bargains.

COACH

There's a YTS Coach Card (ask your supervisor) and a Student Coach Card, if you're at least 16, and a full-time trainee or student. With or without these cards there are fantastic bargains on National Express coaches in the UK, Eurolines around Europe and Greyhound coaches across the USA.

RAIL/SHIP

If you're at least 16 and under 24, or disabled, or have a family, you can get a special Railcard which gives you up to a third off most train fares, and some ferry fares for a year. If you're under 24 you can buy an Inter-Rail Card for cheap travel around 21 European countries from France to Romania, Scandinavia to North Africa. It lasts for one month (if you want to travel for two months, buy two cards). For shorter journeys, for example to France, Belgium or Holland, you can get a youth ticket from an organisation like Transalpino Ltd. If you want to travel around one country you can get a special rover ticket from that country's national railway; but first compare the price with an Inter-Rail Card.

154

AIR

Standby fares are often the cheapest; instead of booking you take a chance there'll be a seat left. Charter, youth and student fares have to be booked a few weeks in advance, but they're far cheaper than ordinary fares.

MOTORBIKE/CAR

Staying alive is better, right? Fun, freedom and safety is what good driving and riding is all about. The trouble is that *young people are often the victims of road accidents, especially on motorbikes and in cars, and especially on Friday and Saturday nights between 9pm and 4am*. The dangers include: speed, alcohol, no seat belt, no crash helmet, inexperience, not looking, too close (should be one yard for every mph), not wearing bright, protective and reflective clothes, tiredness, equipment not checked (tyres, brakes, steering, horn, bell, chain), and not expecting the unexpected.

You can ride a moped (engine under 50cc) at 16, and ride a motorcycle or drive a car at 17:
- if you have a Provisional Licence (application form from any main Post Office)
- if you have insurance (see page 112)
- if you show 'L' plates
- if you have paid road tax
- if you have a driver with a Full Licence with you in a car
- if you ride a motorcycle under 125cc (250cc in Northern Ireland)
- if you have a motorcycle crash helmet (unless you're a Sikh)
- if you don't carry passengers on a motorcycle (unless they have passed their test)

It makes sense to get training from an expert: if you're a rider, ask about the Star Rider Scheme (details from your local motorcycle shop or local authority Road Safety Officer); if you're a driver, get lessons from a *registered* instructor (see Yellow Pages under Driving).

To get a Full Licence you have to take a driving test: for riders a two part test (off the road then on the road); for drivers a one part test (on the road).

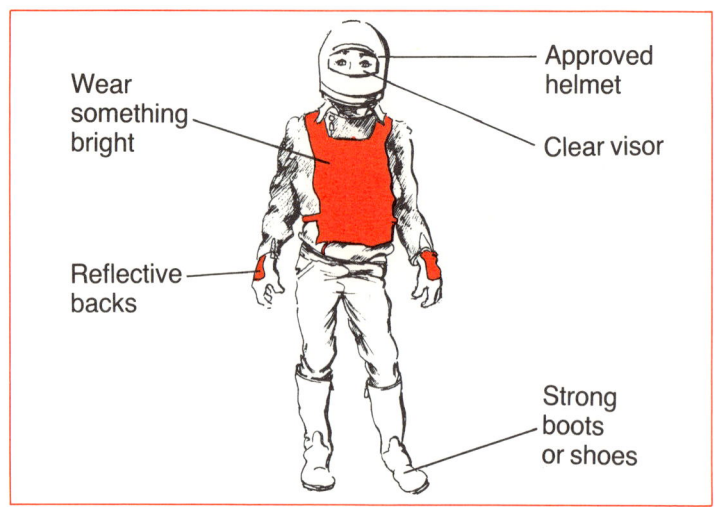

Wear something bright

Approved helmet

Clear visor

Reflective backs

Strong boots or shoes

HITCHHIKING

Not recommended by many travel experts. Are the driver and vehicle safe? Very risky for women travelling alone. Hitch only where the driver can stop safely (never on bends, or at busy junctions).

CONTACTS

■ coach stations and offices
■ large railway stations and rail travel centres
■ any student travel office (at many colleges, polytechnics and universities; they're not just for students); they also have the ISIC card
■ Central Bureau for Educational Visits and Exchanges; they also have the FIYTO Card
■ any travel agent belonging to the Association of British Travel Agents (ABTA – see the ABTA logo on page 157)
■ coach, rail, ferry and air travel companies: if you're disabled let them know your special needs and they'll make your journey a lot easier.

READING

■ books from your local library and bookshop, on safe and cheap travel
■ free leaflets from all coach and railway stations

IDEAS ▶▶▶

The world! France, Spain, Greece, Turkey, Israel and even the USA are possible quite cheaply. It's a pity to miss out. There's so much to discover. Best of all, there are many people to meet. Don't forget to read up all about the UK before you leave, so that you can swop information.

WORKING

You could work on a farm (e.g. picking hops in Kent, grapes in France, apples in Somerset, raspberries in Scotland, peaches in Spain, helping on a communal (kibbutz) farm in Israel), in a hotel in London, on a campsite in France, in a children's holiday camp in the USA, as an au pair in Italy . . . You may have to be at least 16, or 18, or 21. They may pay your fare, give you a free place to stay, and pay you a wage. Obviously it takes several months of organising.

VOLUNTEERING

See page 78.

EXCHANGES/VISITS

To find out about other people, cultures, living conditions, and work-methods in the UK and abroad. You or your school class, youth group or work mates could stay in private homes, youth centres and colleges, for anything from a few days to a year. Obviously it takes a few months of organising.

DO-IT-YOURSELF

For example you could travel around the UK by train with a Railcard, stay in youth hostels, and bring a bike to explore the stops along your route.

157

PACKAGE

There are some good bargains (e.g. to Spain and Greece) with the big tour operators, including special youth holidays. Also look out for fantastic bargains if you are ready to go when and where they send you at the last minute.

ACTIVITY

A holiday plus ballooning, skiing, soccer, tennis, windsurfing, parascending, sailing, surfing, rambling, fossil-finding, chess, computers, astronomy, music, drama... If you are disabled there are plenty of opportunities too: for example the Jubilee Sailing Trust has a special ship for disabled crew.

STUDYING

There are colleges all over the UK and around the world that welcome foreign students for anything from a week to a year or more. The main problem is getting the money to do it. However some UK college courses include periods studying abroad (e.g. Spain, the USA and the Soviet Union).

SPECIAL

The Winston Churchill Memorial Trust offers awards for people to travel to get special experience and knowledge abroad to benefit their work and community.

CONTACTS

- Central Bureau for Educational Visits and Exchanges (CBEVE)
- your national tourist board
- your national Youth Hostel Association (YHA): also ask about activity breaks
- your local PHAB (Physically Handicapped and Able-Bodied) Club
- any travel agent belonging to ABTA
- Outward Bound Trust: adventure in the UK
- Camp America: many opportunities to work in the USA if you're at least 18
- Kibbutz representatives

READING

- *Adventure and Discovery* (Central Bureau for Educational Visits and Exchanges (CBEVE))
- *Adventure Holidays* (Vacation Work Publications (VWP))
- *Summer Jobs in Britain* (VWP)
- *Summer Jobs Abroad* (VWP)
- *Directory of Jobs and Careers Abroad* (VWP)
- *Working Holidays* (CBEVE)
- *Work Your Way Around The World* (VWP)
- books for disabled travellers (Royal Association for Disability and Rehabilitation (RADAR))
- *Kibbutz Volunteer* (VWP)
- *A Year Off* (Careers Research and Advisory Centre (CRAC))
- *Vacation Traineeships* (VWP)
- *Home from Home* (CBEVE): about exchanges

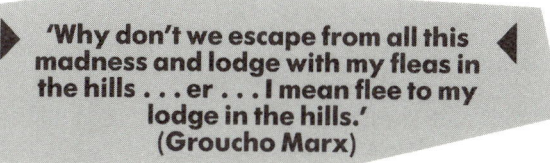

'Why don't we escape from all this madness and lodge with my fleas in the hills . . . er . . . I mean flee to my lodge in the hills.'
(Groucho Marx)

BED ▶▶▶

Cheap doesn't have to mean bad. For example youth hostels, farmhouses and private homes may be much more friendly than expensive hotels, and give you a better chance of meeting people.

IDEAS

- youth hostels: about 400 in the UK and over 5000 youth hostels in Europe and around the world, offering different grades of facilities in, for example, castles, country houses and country cottages; in the country, cities, towns, villages; by the sea, by lakes, and in forests. Some provide meals, some have cooking facilities. All you need is a cheap membership card, special sheet sleeping bag, special guide book and money to pay for each night's stay (about £3)
- camping: borrow tents from friends or buy equipment. Good quality stuff costs more but lasts longer and gives better

service. Campsites offer washing facilities, and some have their own shops. If you camp anywhere else, ask for permission
- guest houses, farmhouses, and private homes. 'Chambre' in France, and 'zimmer' in West Germany
- couchettes on long distance European trains: sleeping compartments with no frills (sharing with 5 others)
- YMCA and YWCA hostels all over the world

CONTACTS
- your national Youth Hostel Association (YHA)
- Central Bureau for Educational Visits and Exchanges (CBEVE)
- the local Tourist Information Office when you arrive (they may phone around and find you a room)
- YMCA
- YWCA
- Camping Club of Great Britain and Ireland

READING
- *Youth Hostel Handbook* for the UK, Europe and the world (Youth Hostel Association (YHA))

READY? ▶▶▶

'Adventure is the result of poor planning!' So says the man who organised Operation Raleigh, the world expedition for young people.

BOOKING

It makes sense to book as much of your journey and accommodation as possible, especially during the hectic summer months.

IDENTIFICATION

At the very least, write your name, address and the telephone numbers of relatives, on the back of an envelope. Official documents are better.

MONEY

Carefully work out how much you need, and how much you've got, and then work out a *realistic* travel budget. It saves a lot of hassle. Take care how you carry money. A money belt is a safe way of keeping small amounts, but for large amounts, travellers' cheques from a bank, Post Office and some travel agents, are much safer. They can be turned into cash in foreign banks and large hotels, but only with your signature, and replaced in under five days if lost or stolen. It also makes sense to bring a small amount of foreign currency for the time before you can cash your travellers' cheques. Order it from a bank well before you leave.

TRAVEL BUDGET

Have
- savings
- loan from parents or bank (see page 112)
and so on

Need
- tickets
- accommodation
- camping equipment
- rucksack
- clothes
- food
- spending money
- insurance
- passport
- maps, sun tan lotion, films, phrase books . . .
and so on

PASSPORT

You can't leave the UK without one. If you're under 18, your parents must agree to you having one. You can get details of how to apply from any main Post Office. Choices:
- British Visitors Passport: for some countries only; lasts one year; issued immediately

161

- British Excursion Document: for France; for trips up to 60 hours only; issued immediately
- Full British Passport: for all countries; it lasts 10 years
- Collective Passport: for a group of 5–50 under 18 years old, with a leader who is at least 21 and has a Full British Passport

VISA

To get into some countries (not EC countries) you need a visa from their London embassy. Details and addresses from a student travel office, or a travel agent. First you may need to prove that you have enough money to cover all the costs of your stay and the cost of your return journey.

FOREIGN CURRENCIES

- Belgium — franc
- Canada — dollar
- France — franc
- Greece — drachma
- Holland — guilder
- Italy — lire
- Norway — kroner
- Portugal — escudo
- Spain — peseta
- Switzerland — franc
- West Germany — deutschmark

INSURANCE

Vital for baggage, money, tickets, and health. See page 112. Health treatment abroad, for example, can cost thousands of pounds. If you're travelling to Belgium, Denmark, France, Greece, Holland, Ireland, Italy, Luxembourg, Portugal, Spain, or West Germany, you should also fill in an E111 Form from your travel agent or your local Department of Health and Social Security (DHSS) Office, before you go, to get cheap medical treatment.

VACCINATIONS

Needed for some countries (not EC countries). See your doctor at least a couple of months before you leave.

SECURITY

Money, cameras, watches, and passports are great favourites of thieves every year. A money belt is a safe way of keeping money. If you keep all expensive possessions in different places, at least you won't lose everything.

SURVIVAL KIT

First aid kit, the right strength of sun tan lotion (vital protection against damaging sun rays), aspirin, diarrhoea tablets, insect repellent (really useful, even in Europe)... Buying these, plus things like maps, films and batteries before you leave will save a lot of money and hassle.

RUCKSACK

A heavy suitcase can be one of your worst holiday memories. A rucksack may be easier to manage than a suitcase, which is heavy even before you pack.

CLOTHES

For warmer places, natural fibres like cotton, instead of artificial fibres like nylon, will keep you cooler and fresher. For colder climates the secret is to bring layers of thin clothes which can be put on or taken off when needed, instead of single bulky sweaters.

LANGUAGE

Many of us expect 'foreigners' to understand English, and then we shout louder in English when they don't. A few hours spent listening to language records/cassettes from your local library or taking an evening course at a local college, or just reading a phrase book, could make your stay a lot more fun. And making the effort to speak a language, even badly, earns you respect abroad.

✍ READING

- *Europe by Train* (Fontana)
- *British Rail International Passenger Timetable*
- *Traveller's Survival Kit Europe* (Vacation Work Publications (VWP))
- *Disabled International Phrasebook* (Disability Press)
- *Traveller's Handbook* (WEXAS): tells you everything you need to know
- *Medical Costs Abroad: What You Need To Know* and *Protect Your Health Abroad (free leaflet, from main Post Offices and your local Department of Health and Social Security (DHSS) Office)*

LAW

LAWS
POLICE
COURTS
HELP
UNFAIR?

For every right to freedom, there is a responsibility not to hurt others.

LAWS ▶▶▶

Laws are made by Parliament, or by local councils (by-laws) with the approval of Parliament. There are many differences in Scotland and Northern Ireland.

Civil law is about private matters, such as disputes between buyers and sellers, employees and employers, landlords and tenants, husbands and wives, neighbours, owners and trespassers, which affect only the people involved.

All addresses in Addresses!

Criminal law is about public matters: vandalism, theft, attack, which affect all of us.

Laws are mentioned throughout this book, because there are so many of them. Some are quite well known, such as the Sex Discrimination Act, Race Relations Act, Health and Safety at Work Act, Police and Criminal Evidence Act, Equal Pay Act and Rent Acts.

At 18 you are seen to be fully responsible for your actions under civil law, and at 17 fully responsible under criminal law. However under 21 you get special treatment under the law:

13
- you can do light work, but for no more than two hours per day

15
- you can go to a '15' film, if you can prove your age

16
- you can leave school. Under 16, you must have full-time education, but that be could be outside school, if your Education Authority agrees in writing
- you can leave home if your parents or a court agree (in Scotland you don't need their agreement)
- you can drink (but not buy) beer, cider or wine with a meal in a pub or restaurant (18 in Northern Ireland)
- girls can have sex (17 in Northern Ireland)
- you can get married if your parents or a court agree (in Scotland you don't need their agreement)
- you can work full-time
- you can join a trade union
- you can choose your own doctor
- you can get your own passport with your parents' agreement.
- you can claim any benefits
- you can ride a moped
- you can choose your own religion

17
- you can ride a motorcycle or drive a car

18
- you can leave home
- you can get married
- you can vote

- you can buy alcohol
- you can sign contracts (so you can do a lot of things)
- you can go to an '18' film

21
- you can drive a lorry (Heavy Goods Vehicle)
- you can stand as a candidate for local, UK and European elections

CONTACTS
- Children's Legal Centre: information on how laws affect young people
- National Council for Civil Liberties (NCCL)
- Scottish Council for Civil Liberties

READING
- *First Rights: A Guide to Legal Rights for Young People* (National Council for Civil Liberties (NCCL))
- *Penguin Guide to the Law* (Penguin)

POLICE ▶▶▶

The police have to enforce the law, but they don't make it, or have a final decision on whether people have broken it. They are also there to help.

The police can:
- stop and search you if they suspect you of carrying drugs, weapons or stolen goods; if you refuse to be searched you could be arrested
- question you at the police station, if you agree to go and help them with their enquiries; if you refuse you could be arrested (but unless you have been arrested, you can leave at any time)
- arrest you: they must say that you are 'under arrest' and tell you why; if they hold you for more than a certain number of hours (normally 24, but check with your solicitor) they must either release you or charge you
- charge you with committing a crime: you can ask to go home on 'bail' to wait until your court case; the police may refuse bail or they may ask for money (from you or someone on your behalf) and promises that you'll turn up in court

167

You should:
- stay cool and polite
- say nothing apart from giving your name, address and age until you have a solicitor with you
- contact a solicitor, who will stop you saying or doing the wrong thing: if you don't have your own solicitor ask for the emergency (duty) solicitor, or if there isn't one, ask to see the list of solicitors kept at the police station
- if you are under 17, insist on your right not to be questioned without a parent, solicitor, adult friend, youth worker or social worker being with you
- never, under any circumstances, admit to a crime you didn't do

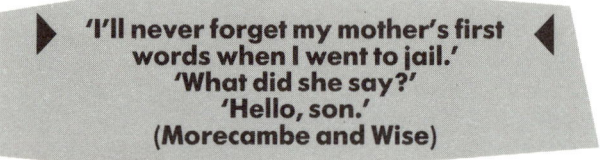

'I'll never forget my mother's first words when I went to jail.'
'What did she say?'
'Hello, son.'
(Morecambe and Wise)

COURTS ▶▶▶

Courts have to decide whether people have broken the law, and on the penalty if they have broken it.

Always get expert help with a court case, from a Citizens Advice Bureau, Law Centre, or solicitor.

TRIBUNALS

Much more relaxed than other courts:
- Industrial Tribunals for disputes about employment rights
- Social Security Appeal Tribunals for disputes about whether someone can get benefits
- Immigration Tribunals for disputes about whether someone can stay in the UK

and so on.

CIVIL

- Small Claims Courts for disputes involving amounts up to £500

- County Courts for disputes involving amounts up to £5000
- High Courts for disputes involving larger amounts and other cases such as custody (see page 125) and misuse of power by government departments

CRIMINAL

- Juvenile Courts for people under 17. Relaxed and using simple language. There are magistrates (trained local people) carefully chosen because they care about young people. The penalties (sentences) don't include prison
- Magistrates' Courts for most other cases. There are three magistrates
- Crown Courts for more serious cases. There's a judge, and a jury of 12 people chosen at random (could be anyone, including you if you're at least 18 and asked to do 'jury service'). The jury decides whether or not a person is guilty, but the judge decides on the penalty

APPEAL

If you feel badly treated by a court, you may be able to appeal to other courts, in this order:
- the Court of Appeal
- the House of Lords
- an international court (see page 179)

PENALTIES

- fines for civil offences
- fines, bans, cautions, supervision orders (supervised by a social worker), community service, Youth Custody (YC), Detention Centre (DC), jail (at 21) for criminal offences

H E L P ▶▶▶

Obviously it's better to avoid a situation where you would become involved with the law. That means keeping out of trouble, double-checking documents before signing them, keeping all important letters and documents, keeping your belongings in a safe place, never walking alone down unlit pathways.

169

But sometimes you may have to get involved in legal matters, and may need help from a legal expert; for example:

- if you are having trouble with a landlord
- if you are hurt in an accident
- if you are discriminated against because of your race or sex, perhaps when choosing school subjects, applying for a job or youth training
- if you are arrested

and so on.

Remember that no-one and no organisation is above the law, not even your school, the police, or government departments.

Never be afraid to get help. Ask to speak to an expert specialising in your problem. Your local Citizens Advice Bureau (trained staff) and Law Centre (qualified solicitors) charge nothing. Solicitors may charge (ask how much *before* your interview, and say if you can't afford the fee), but try to get:

- free information or advice under the Green Form Scheme (or if you can't get this, ask for a Fixed Fee Interview (half an hour for £5))
- free or cheap help under the Legal Aid Scheme (see the Legal Aid logo below) if you (or your parents if you're under 16) don't have much money

CONTACTS

- any solicitor offering Legal Aid (look for the Legal Aid sticker in the window)

READING

- *Solicitors' Regional Directory*: lists all local solicitors (see it at your local library or Citizens Advice Bureau)

U N F A I R ? ▶▶▶

Law isn't always the same thing as justice, but you can take action under the law to try to get justice.

LAW

Take action to try and get it changed by Parliament (see page 175).

POLICE

Get advice from your local Citizens Advice Bureau, Law Centre, youth workers and community leaders.

COURT

Ask your solicitor whether you should appeal.

SOLICITOR

Contact the Law Society, and in the meantime get help from another solicitor.

ACTION

Bob Geldof was outraged by TV pictures of starving people in Ethiopia. He rang Midge Ure, Simon le Bon, Sting . . . and Band Aid was born. Together they raised tens of millions of pounds, and saved many lives.

Whether it's a campaign to help a toad across the road, or to fight for justice, you CAN take peaceful action and get results.

WHY ▶▶▶

'Man who sits in middle of road gets hit by chariots going both ways,' said the Chinese philosopher Confucius 2500 years ago. Many of the things we take for granted today, such as the vote, free health treatment, rights at work, benefits, and protection of plants and animals, are the result of action by people who weren't prepared to put up with things they thought were wrong.

172

All addresses in addresses!

Politics is about life, and the issues affecting all of us, directly or indirectly. It's not just something 'done' by a small group of people in Parliament, arguing about the economy. Politics includes policy- and decision-making in schools, hospitals, work places, local communities and regions. And in Parliament, and in the Government, decisions are being made affecting issues such as youth training, health care, conservation, aid for the Third World, benefits, nuclear weapons.

Not only is it your life that's being affected, it's your money the politicians are spending! You pay for government every time you pay tax on the things you buy in the shops, or on the money you earn. You have as much right to a say, and to take action, as anyone else.

FACTS?

'Sexy Susie's Saucy Sauna' may be what people want to read about, but is that sort of 'news' true, or important, or insulting to women, or better wrapped round fish and chips? No facts, no comment.

OPINIONS

Everyone's background gives them different experiences of the 'real' world, and different opinions that matter as much as anyone else's. Tolerating, listening to, and trying to understand these opinions are the keys to a peaceful neighbourhood, country and world.

POLITICS

Politics is supposed to be the art of the possible, but often seems to be the art of promising the impossible. Clever speeches don't pay for policies, or avoid their harmful effects. For example if government spending on defence goes up, spending on hospitals may have to come down; if government spends more to cut unemployment, it may push up inflation (prices).

ISSUES?

- are prison sentences tough enough?
- should people have to work for their benefits?
- should young people be forced to do military service?
- is there too much welfare, and not enough wealth creation?
- is the Soviet Union an enemy?
- is there too much confrontation, and not enough co-operation between people?
- should all schools be allowed to elect pupil governors?
- what can be done about our depressed inner-city areas?
- should important industries be privatised or nationalised (see page 60)?
- is it safe to have, or not have, nuclear weapons?
- should some councils be allowed to overspend their budgets to provide social services?
- does the government have too much control over our lives?
- is America likely to drag us into a war or keep us out of one?
- is it better to have stronger government through our present 'first past the post' voting system (winner takes all), or fairer government through a 'proportional representation system' (which gives parties a share of seats closer to their share of votes)?
- what, if anything, can be done to fight, or at least cope with, youth unemployment?
- is there enough power outside London, for people in Scotland, Wales, Northern Ireland, the West Country, and the north of England to control their own lives?
- what should be done about unfair treatment because of sex and race, and also because of age, religion, colour, disability, marriage and beliefs?
- if you can marry, leave school, get benefits etc. at 16, should you be allowed to vote at 16?
- are we too obsessed by economic growth instead of protecting our limited resources on earth?
- are government job schemes just a way to hide the real employment figures?
- should there be a 'basic wage' for everyone, including children, instead of benefits, to take account of long-term unemployment and the importance of volunteering as a way of working?
- is nuclear power safe?
- is it important that every day, one or more plant/animal species becomes extinct?

174

- should part-time workers have more rights?
- is the UK seriously divided: between a poor north and a rich south, the employed and the unemployed, black and white, management and workers?
- would the use of nuclear weapons be a crime against humanity?
- is there enough protection of land, water and air from things like chemical pollution and development?
- should we do more to help the two thirds of the world living in hunger and misery?

and so on.

DO IT YOURSELF!

Organising (see page 151), complaining (see page 116), using the law (see page 170), appealing (see page 168), volunteering (see page 78) . . .

USING REPRESENTATIVES

'If you've got half a mind to go into politics, that's all you need!' Well that's one opinion anyway. But whatever you think of them, and whether you vote for them or not, your elected representatives (see page 178) must represent you. They are more likely to help if you can show them that you have a group of voters, or future voters, behind you, and that you've researched your case thoroughly. Write to them or visit them (names and addresses from your local library).

NEWSPAPERS, RADIO, TV

The media need stories. You can write to a newspaper editor or radio/TV producer (or send a film/video) with your views or news. Your letter may be printed or you may be interviewed on radio/TV, or helped to make your own programme.

PETITION

What about a questionnaire or petition to find out what local people think about an issue? You could collect signatures and send them to your representatives.

PRESSURE GROUP

You name it, there's a pressure group for it. If you write to a group's headquarters, they'll put you in touch with a local branch. Examples:

- Amnesty International (to help non-violent political prisoners)
- British Youth Council
- Disability Alliance
- Friends of the Earth (protecting the environment)
- Life (anti-abortion)
- Oxfam (aid for the Third World)
- Royal Society for the Prevention of Cruelty to Animals (RSPCA)

and so on.

PARTY

You can join a local branch and discuss the local, UK, European and world issues, stand for election, campaign, and go to meetings of special groups within the party (e.g. for young people or women). It's a great opportunity to make friends too. Examples:

- Conservative Party
- Democratic Unionist Party (DUP) (Northern Ireland)
- Labour Party
- Official Unionist Party (Northern Ireland)
- Plaid Cymru (Wales)
- Scottish National Party (SNP) (Scotland)
- Social and Liberal Democratic Party (SLDP)
- Social Democratic and Labour Party (SDLP) (Northern Ireland)

VOTING

'Democracy is the worst form of government except for all those other forms that have been tried'. So said Winston Churchill. At 18 you can vote in:

- local council elections, held at least every four years
- UK Parliament elections, held at least every five years
- European Parliament elections, held at least every five years.

You can vote along with other people living in your local council ward or parliamentary constituency. To vote, your name must be on the Electoral Register. A form is sent to each household every autumn asking if you want to join the register. Apply when you're 17, so that you can vote as soon as you're 18.

176

At voting time you are sent a Polling Card which you exchange for a voting paper at your local Polling Station (usually a local school or hall). Take the voting paper to a private booth and put an X next to the candidate of your choice, then pop the voting paper into the black voting box. If you are disabled or living away from home you can apply to vote by post.

STANDING

Could be a good way to find out what a politician can and can't do! Why not stand for election to school or college posts? Or trade union posts at 16? Or for election as a local councillor, Member of Parliament, or Member of the European Parliament at 21? You may have more success as a member of a party.

CONTACTS
■ your local library (name and address of any political organisation)

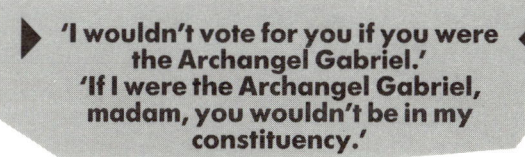

> 'I wouldn't vote for you if you were the Archangel Gabriel.'
> 'If I were the Archangel Gabriel, madam, you wouldn't be in my constituency.'

WHERE ▶▶▶

GRASSROOTS

You can ask class, school, trade union, college, and community representatives to represent your opinions about facilities, safety, conditions, grants, pay and so on. There are all sorts of grass-roots bodies:
■ school councils
■ school boards of governors
■ works committees
■ trade unions
■ tenants associations
■ community councils
■ community relations councils (for racial problems)
■ student councils
■ college councils
and so on.

177

LOCAL

You can ask your local councillor to represent your opinions about housing, recreation facilities, bin-emptying, environmental health (district councils), and transport, roads, schools, social work (county/regional councils). There are some differences in Scotland and Northern Ireland, though. Local government is made up of:

- councillors elected to decide on local issues. You can see your local councillors in action by sitting in the public gallery of your local council chamber
- officials who are non-elected council employees, carrying out council policies in the local Education Department, Housing Department, Social Services Department, Planning Department, Leisure Services Department, etc.

UK

You can ask your local Member of Parliament (MP) to represent your opinions about matters such as UK laws, education, defence, benefits, taxes, UK overseas aid, prisons and unemployment. The main UK bodies are:

- Parliament, made up of elected MPs sitting in the House of Commons, and non-elected Lords in the House of Lords: members of either House can introduce proposals (Bills) for laws (Acts), and they can also question the Government. Parliament is far more powerful in the UK than most of the other bodies mentioned in this chapter. You can see and hear Parliament in action on radio and TV every weekday, or by going to London and sitting in the public galleries of the Palace of Westminster
- Government, usually formed from the largest party in the House of Commons, or a union (coalition) of parties to make the largest group. The Government makes most of the day-to-day decisions affecting the whole of the UK: The leader of the largest party becomes Prime Minister and leading party members from the Commons or Lords become Secretaries of State or Ministers, in charge of government Departments for Education, Employment, Agriculture, Scotland, Wales, Northern Ireland, etc. Together they meet as the Cabinet.
- Civil Service of non-elected government employees, carrying out Government policy in the government departments
- Courts which enforce laws

178

EUROPE

You can ask your Member of the European Parliament (MEP) to represent your opinions about European law, fishing, farming, pollution, regional development, human rights, etc. The members of the European Community (EC) are Belgium, Denmark, France, Greece, Holland, Ireland, Italy, Luxembourg, Portugal, Spain, UK and West Germany. The EC may be the beginning of a United States of Europe (similar to the USA and USSR) eventually having its own bank notes, and defence and laws. The main EC bodies are:

- European Parliament in Strasbourg, with MEPs from all over the EC
- European Council of Ministers in Brussels, made up of EC Foreign Ministers.
- European Commission in Brussels
- European Court of Justice in Luxembourg, for settling disputes between states. There is also a European Commission on Human Rights which may help you with a human rights issue, but only after you have tried every other means of getting justice in the UK

United Nations

WORLD

You can ask your MP to represent your opinions about world disarmament, refugees, health, aid for the Third World, human rights, development, youth issues, environmental issues, women's issues. There are many actors on the world stage, including national governments, multi-national companies, and international organisations, but the one which has members from nearly every country of the world is the United Nations (UN). The UN's main purpose is to keep world peace, but it deals with just about any issue affecting all peoples of the world. Its greatest success has been the wiping out of smallpox, a disease which used to kill millions of people. It is only as powerful as its members want it to be (which usually means not very powerful!) but it may become far more important in the future as we become more of a global village. The main UN bodies include:

- UN General Assembly in New York: the nearest thing to a world parliament, with ambassadors from each country. Each country has one vote, no matter what its size
- UN Security Council in New York, ready to meet at any time, whenever peace is threatened. Its members always include ambassadors from China, France, the Soviet Union, the UK and the United States
- UN Secretariat in several centres (e.g. New York and Geneva), and 'in the field' around the world. It's an international civil service, headed by the Secretary General of the United Nations
- International Court of Justice, for settling disputes between states

There are also UN agencies, organs and forces, such as:
- UNICEF (United Nations Children's Fund)
- FAO (Food and Argiculture Organisation of the United Nations)
- UNESCO (United Nations Educational, Scientific and Cultural Organisation)
- WHO (World Health Organisation)
- UNIFIL (United Nations Interim Force in Lebanon)

The money spent on the work of the UN each year is about half the amount the world spends on weapons — every day.

CONTACTS
- your nearest European Commission Information Office
- United Nations Association (UNA) (you can join, and go to your local UNA meetings)
- United Nations Information Centre (UNIC)

READING
- *Your United Nations* (from HMSO bookshops)
- *The United Nations for Young People: Hope for Tomorrow* (from United Nations Information Centre)

Our World, Our Future

Young people everywhere are aspiring to a world of justice and opportunity. They are seeking remedies to the poverty that besets much of mankind and an end to the arms race.

Javier Pérez de Cuéllar Secretary-General of the United Nations

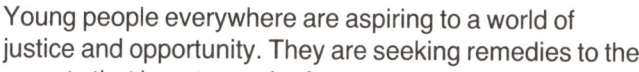

Addresses!

When writing to any organisation don't forget to send and SAE (see page 32).

Advisory Services for Squatters
2 St Paul's Road
London N1
01 359 8814

Alcoholics Anonymous
11 Redcliffe Gardens
London SW10 9BQ
01 352 9779

Amnesty International
Tower House
8–14 Southampton Street
London WC2
01 838 5621

Anorexic Aid
The Priory Centre
11 Priory Road
High Wycombe
Buckinghamshire

Apex Trust
Brixton Hill Place
London SW2 1HJ
01 671 7633

Arts Councils
Arts Council of Great Britain
105 Piccadilly
London W1V 0AU
01 629 9495

Arts Council of Northern Ireland
181a Stranmills Road
Belfast BT9 5DU
0232 381591

Scottish Arts Council
19 Charlotte Square
Edinburgh
031 226 6051

Welsh Arts Council
Holst House
Museum Place
Cardiff CF1 3NX
0222 394711

Associated Examining Board (AEB)
Stag Hill House
Guildford
Surrey GU2 5XJ
0483 506506

Black and In Care
20 Compton Terrace
London N1 2UN
01 226 7102

British Pregnancy Advisory Service (BPAS)
58 Petit France
London SW1
01 222 0985

245 North Street
Glasgow G3 7DL
041 204 1832

4 High Street
Arcade Chambers
Cardiff CF1 2BE
0222 43820

British Red Cross
9 Grosvenor Crescent
London SW1X 7EJ
01 235 5454

British Trust for Conservation Volunteers
36 St Mary's Street
Wallingford
Oxfordshire
0491 39766

British Volunteer Programme
22 Coleman Fields
London N1 7AG
01 226 6616

British Youth Council
57 Chalton Street
London NW1 1HU
01 387 7559

Brook Advisory Centres
153a East Street
London SE17 2SD
01 708 1234

2 Lower Gilmore Place
Edinburgh EH3 9NY
031 229 3596

21 Richmond Hill
Bristol BS8 1BA
0272 736657

183

Business and Technical Education Council (BTEC)
Central House
Upper Woburn Place
London WC1H 0HH
01 388 3288

Camp America
37 Queen's Gate
London SW7
01 589 3223

Camping Club of Great Britain and Ireland
(Youth Section)
11 Grosvenor Place
London SW1W 0EY
01 828 1012

Careers and Occupational Information Centre (COIC)
Manpower Services
Commission
Moorfoot
Sheffield S1 4PQ
0742 704 563

Careers Research and Advisory Centre (CRAC)
Hobsons Press Ltd.
Bateman Street
Cambridge CB2 1LZ
0223 354551

Central Bureau for Educational Visits and Exchanges (CBEVE)
Seymour Mews House
Seymour Mews
London W1H 9PE
01 486 5101

3 Bruntsfield Gardens
Edinburgh EH10 4HD
031 447 8024

16 Malone Road
Belfast BT9 5BN
0232 664418

Childline
Freepost 1111
London EC4B 4BB
Freephone 0800 1111

Children's Legal Centre
20 Compton Terrace
London 01 359 6251

City and Guilds of London Institute (CGLI)
46 Britannia Street
London WC1X 9RG
01 278 2468

Community Service Volunteers
237 Pentonville Road
London N1 9NJ
01 278 6601

90 West Nile Street
Glasgow G2
041 331 2375

22 High Street
Belfast BT1 2BD
0232 321946

Conservative Party
32 Smith Square
London SW1P 3HH
01 222 9000

Co-operative Development Agency
Broadmead House
21 Panton Street
London SW1Y 4DR
01 839 2988

Canada House
22 North Street
Belfast BT1 1LA
0232 232755

Templeton Street
Glasgow G40 1DA
041 554 3797

Council for the Accreditation of Correspondence Colleges (CACC)
27 Marylebone Road
London NW1 5JS
01 935 5391

Council for Small Industries in Rural Areas (CoSIRA)
141 Castle Street
Salisbury
Wiltshire SP1 3TP
0722 336255

Council for Wales of Voluntary Youth Services
5 Washington Chambers
Stanwell Road
Penarth
South Glamorgan
CF6 2AF
0222 705611

Democratic Unionist Party
296 Albert Bridge Road
Belfast
0232 58597

DHSS Leaflets Unit
PO Box 21
Stanmore
Middlesex HA7 1AY
01 952 2311

Disability Alliance
25 Denmark Street
London WC2H 8NJ
01 240 0806

Duke of Edinburgh's Award Scheme
5 Prince of Wales
Terrace
Kensington
London W8 5PG
01 937 5205

69 Dublin Street
Edinburgh EH3 6NS
031 556 9097

17 Cathedral Road
Cardiff
0222 28570

593 Lisburn Road
Belfast BT9 7GS
0232 667123

Educational Guidanc Service
Eldon House
Regent Centre
Newcastle-upon-Tyne
NE3 3PW
091 984 1611

Bryson House
28 Bedford Street
Belfast BT2 7FE
0232 244274

74 Victoria Crescent
Road
Glasgow G12 9JO
041 357 1774

Adult Education Office
Rhyl High School
Grange Road
Rhyl
0745 31609

Empty Property Unit
157 Waterloo Road
London SE1
01 633 9377

Eurolines
International Express
237–239 Oxford Street
London W1R 1AB
01 439 9368

European Commission Information Office
8 Storey's Gate
London SW1P 3AT
01 222 8122

Windsor House
9/15 Bedford Street
Belfast
BT2 7EG
0232 24078

4 Cathedral Road
Cardiff
CF1 9SG
0222 371631

7 Alva Street
Edinburgh
EH2 2PH
031 225 2058

European Commission on Human Rights
Council of Europe
Strasbourg
67006
FRANCE
010 33 88 614 961

Family Planning Association
27 Mortimer Street
London
W1N 7RJ
01 636 7866

4 Clifton Street
Glasgow
G3 7LA
041 333 9696

113 University Street
Belfast
BT7 1HP
0232 225488

Family Planning Information Service
27–35 Mortimer Street
London
W1N 7RJ
01 636 7866

Friends of the Earth
377 City Road
London
EC1V 1NA
01 837 0731

Gamblers Anonymous/Young Gamblers
17–23 Blantyre Street
London
SW10
01 352 3060

Gay Switchboard
01 837 7324

Instant Muscle
Haymill Centre
112 Burnham Lane
Burnham
Slough
SL1 6LZ
06286 63926

International Voluntary Service
53 Regent Road
Leicester
LE1 6YL
0533 541862

Jubilee Sailing Trust
Atlantic Road
Eastern Docks
Southampton
0703 631 388

Kibbitz Representatives
1 Accommodation Road
London
NW11
01 485 9235

Labour Party
150 Walworth Road
London
SE17 1JT
01 703 0833

Law Society
113 Chancery Lane
London
WC2A 1PL
01 242 1222

Law Society for Scotland
26 Drumsheugh Gardens
Edinburgh
EH3 7YR
031 226 7411

Law Society for Northern Ireland
90 Victoria Street
Belfast
BT1 3GN
0232 231614

**Lesbian and Gay
Youth Movement**
London
WC1N 3XX
01 317 9690

Liberal Party
1 Whitehall Place
London
SW1A 2HA
01 839 0492

LIFE
118 Warwick Street
Leamington
Warwickshire
CV32 4QY
0926 21587

Livewire
Livewire Freepost
Newton Mearns
Glasgow G77 5BR
041 639 1919

Livewire Freepost
Cardiff CF1 1YW
0227 494411

Livewire Freepost
Belfast BT7 1BR
0232 234 504/231730

Livewire Freepost
Newcastle upon Tyne
NE1 1BR
091 261 5584

**Local Enterprise
Development Unit
(LEDU)**
Upper Galwally
Belfast
BT8 4TB
0232 691031

**Marriage Guidance
Councils**
Herbert Gray College
Little Church Street
Rugby
Warwickshire
CV21 3AP
0788 73241

26 Frederick Street
Edinburgh
EH2 2JR
031 225 5006

76 Dublin Road
Belfast
BT2 7HP
0232 223454

**Message Home
Service**
01 799 7662

**National Association
for the Care and
Resettlement of
Offenders (NACRO)**
169 Clapham Road
London
SW9 0PU
01 582 6500

*Scottish Association
(SACRO)*
53 George Street
Edinburgh 2
031 226 4222

*Northern Ireland
Association (NIACRO)*
22 Adelaide Street
Belfast
BT2 8GD
0232 320157

**National Association
of Young People in
Care**
20 Compton Terrace
London
N1 2UN
01 226 7102

**National Bureau for
Handicapped
Students (NBHS)**
336 Brixton Road
London
SW9 7AA
01 274 0565

**National Council for
Civil Liberties**
21 Tabard Street
London
SE1 4LA
01 403 3888

**National Council for
One-Parent Families**
255 Kentish Town Road
London
NW5 2LX
01 267 1361

**National Extension
College**
18 Brooklands Avenue
Cambridge
CB2 2HN
0223 316644

**National Society for
the Prevention of
Cruelty to Children
(NSPCC)**
67 Saffron Hill
London
EC1N 8RS
01 242 1626

**National Union of
Students (NUS)**
461 Holloway Road
London
N7 6LJ
01 272 8900

11 Fitzwilliam Street
Belfast
BT9 6AW
0232 244641

12 Dublin Street
Edinburgh
EH1 3PP
031 556 6598

107 Walter Road
Swansea
SA1 5QQ
0792 43323

National Youth Bureau (NYB)
17–23 Albion Street
Leicester
LE1 6GD
0533 554775

National Youth Theatre
32 York Way
London
N1 9AB
01 837 0118

New Grapevine
416 St John Street
London
EC1
01 278 9147

Ocean Youth Club
c/o The Bus Station
South Street
Gosport
Hampshire PO12 1EP
0705 528421

Official/Ulster Unionist Party
3 Glengall Street
Belfast 12
0232 324601

Open College
Freepost
PO Box 35
Abingdon OX14 3BR
0235 555 444

Open University
Walton Hall
Milton Keynes
Buckinghamshire
MK7 6AA
0908 74066

Outward Bound Trust
Chestnut Field
Regent Place
Rugby
CV21 2PJ
0788 60423

Oxfam
274 Banbury Road
Oxford
OX2 7DZ
0865 56777

Parents Anonymous
6 Manor Gardens
London
N7 6LA
01 263 8918

Physically Handicapped and Able Bodied (PHAB)
Tavistock House North
Tavistock Square
London
WC1H 9HJ
01 388 1963

Piccadilly Advice Centre
Subway 4
Piccadilly Underground Station
London
W1
01 930 0066

Plaid Cymru
51 Cathedral Street
(Heol yr Eglwys)
Cardiff
CF1 9HD
0222 31944

Practical Action
Victoria Chambers
16–20 Strutton Ground
London
SW1P 2HP
01 222 3341

The Prince's Youth Business Trust
8 Jockey's Fields
London WC1R 4TJ
01 430 0521

Project Fullemploy
102 Park Village East
London
NW1 3SP
01 387 1222

Rape Crisis Centre
PO Box 69
London WC1X 9NJ
01 837 1600

Royal Association for Disability and Rehabilitation (RADAR)
25 Mortimer Street
London W1N 8AB
01 637 5400

Royal Jubilee Trusts
8 Bedford Row
London WC1R 4BA
01 430 0524

Royal Society for the Prevention of Cruelty to Animals (RSPCA)
Causeway
Horsham
Sussex RH12 1HG
0403 64181

Royal Society of Arts
John Adam Street
Adelphi
London WC2N 6EZ
01 930 5115

Scottish Community Education Council
Atholl House
2 Canning Street
Edinburgh EH3 8EG
031 229 2433

Scottish Council for Civil Liberties (SCCL)
146 Holland Street
Glasgow G2 4NG
041 332 5960

Scottish Development Agency
Rosebery House
Haymarket Terrace
Edinburgh EH12 5EZ
031 337 9595

Scottish Education Department (SED)
Haymarket House
Clifton Terrace
Edinburgh EH12 5DR
031 556 8400

Scottish National Party (SNP)
6 North Charlotte Street
Edinburgh EH2 4JH
031 226 3661

Scottish Vocational Education Council (SCOTVEC)
38 Queen Street
Glasgow G1 3DY
041 248 7900

Scottish Youth Theatre
48 Albany St.
Edinburgh EH1 3QR
031 557 2224

Shelter
157 Waterloo Road
London SE1 8XF
01 633 9377

65 Cockburn Street
Edinburgh EH1 1BU
031 226 6347

23a University Road
Belfast BT7 1NA
0232 247752

57 Walter Road
Swansea
0792 469400

Small Firms Service
Ashdown House
123 Victoria Street
London SW1E 6RB
Freephone Enterprise

Social Democratic Party (SDP)
4 Cowley Street
London SW1 3NB
01 222 7999

Social Democratic and Labour Party (SDLP)
38 University Street
Belfast 7
0232 323428

Sports Council
16 Upper Woburn Place
London WC1
01 388 1277

Scottish Sports Council
1 St Colme Street
Edinburgh EH3 6AA
031 225 8411

Sports Council for Northern Ireland
House of Sport
Upper Malone Road
Belfast BT9 5LA
0232 661222

Sports Council for Wales
Sophia Gardens
Cardiff CF1 9SW
0222 397571

Tourist Boards
English Tourist Board
Thames Tower
Black's Road
London W6 9EL
01 846 9000

Northern Ireland Tourist Board
River House
48 High Street
Belfast BT1 2DF
0232 231221

Scottish Tourist Board
23 Ravelston Terrace
Edinburgh EH4 3EU
031 332 2433

Welsh Tourist Board
Brunel House
2 Fitzalan Road
Cardiff CF2 1UY
0222 499909

Trades Union Congress
Congress House
Great Russell Street
London WC1 3LS
01 636 4030

Transalpino
71–75 Buckingham Palace Road
London SW1
01 834 9656

11 Snow Hill
Queensway
Birmingham
021 236 2507/236 7469

150 West George Street
Glasgow
041 333 9177

24 Lombard Street
Belfast
0232 248823

Ulster Pregnancy Advisory Association
719a Lisburn Road
Belfast 0232 667345

United Nations Association (UNA)
3 Whitehall Court
London SW1A 2EL
01 930 2931

United Nations Information Centre (UNIC)
20 Buckingham Gate
London SW1E 6LB
01 630 1981

Vacation Work Publications (VWP)
9 Park End Street
Oxford OX1 1HJ
0865 241978

Voluntary Service Overseas
9 Belgrave Square
London SW1X 8PW
01 235 5191

Welsh Development Agency (WDA)
Glantaf House
Treforest Industrial Estate
Pontypridd
Mid Glamorgan
CF37 5UT
044 385 2666

Winston Churchill Memorial Trust
15 Queen's Gate Terrace
London SW7 5PR
01 584 9315

Workers' Educational Association (WEA)
9 Upper Berkeley Street
London W1H 8BY
01 402 5608

YMCA National Council
640 Forest Road
London E17 3DZ
01 520 5599

Young Enterprise
Robert Hyde House
48 Bryanston Square
London W1H 1BQ
01 724 7641

Young Farmers' Clubs Federation
YFC Centre
National Agriculture Centre
Kenilworth
Warwickshire
CV8 2LG
0203 56131

Youth Business Trust
8 Bedford Row
London WC1R 4BA
01 430 0521

Youth Club Associations
National Association of Youth Clubs
Keswick House
70 St Nicholas Circle
Leicester LE1 5NY
0533 29514

Scottish Association of Youth Clubs
Balfour House
17 Bonnington Grove
Edinburgh EH6 4DP
031 554 2561

Northern Ireland Association of Youth Clubs
Hampton
Glenmachan Park
Belfast BT4 2PJ
0232 760067

Welsh Association of Youth Clubs
Andrews Buildings
67 Queen Street
Cardiff CF1 4AW
0222 20396/7

Youth Enterprise Scheme
16/20 Strutton Ground
London SW1P 2HP
01 222 3341

Youth Hostels
Youth Hostels Association (YHA)
Trevelyan House
8 St Stephens Hill
St Albans
Herts AL1 2DY
0727 55215

Scottish Youth Hostels Association
7 Glebe Crescent
Stirling FK8 2JA
0786 72821

Youth Hostel Association of Northern Ireland
56 Bradbury Place
Belfast BT7 1RU
0232 324733

Youth Information Service
86 Lisburn Road
Belfast BT9 6AF
0232 681447

YWCA National Offices
Clarendon House
52 Cornmarket St
Oxford OX1 3EJ
0865 726110

The Basic Skills Series

These straightforward, practical and attractive books are designed for use in connection with the AEB's Basic Tests, or for any skills development with students of 14+, including those of TVEI courses. They cover literacy, numeracy and other basic competencies, essential skills for school leavers looking for jobs.

English by Paul Groves and Nigel Grimshaw

The authors cover the practical use of good English in a variety of situations, mainly work-related. The *Students' Book* covers topics such as taking notes, writing formal letters, applying for jobs and answering the telephone. The *Teachers' Resource Book* contains dictation passages and copyright-waived worksheet material.

Students' Book 0 7195 4350 9

Teachers' Resource Book 0 7195 4351 7

Arithmetic by John Deft

The *Students' Book* emphasises the understanding of principles, and gives practice in skills such as problem-solving, estimating and interpreting data. The *Teachers' Resource Book* provides answers, additional exercises, revision papers and puzzles in copyable form.

Students' Book 0 7195 4349 5

Teachers' Resource Book 0 7195 5346 8

Electronics by Tom Duncan

This book is intended for all who want to gain knowledge and understanding of the basic principles of electronics, and is suitable for anyone taking an introductory course at school, college or at home. It includes basic theory, questions, and full instructions for experiments and projects.

0 7195 4449 1

Health, Hygiene and Safety by Di Barton and Wilf Stout

The three highly illustrated sections of this book provide excellent grounding in important areas of health science. They cover topics such as: how the body works, food preparation and hygiene, protection from hazards in the home and at work.

0 7195 4463 7

Science by Peter Leckstein

The emphasis of this book is on applications of basic science. The six highly illustrated sections are: keeping fit, keeping warm, keeping mobile, keeping fed, keeping sheltered, keeping in touch.

0 7195 4445 9